Gamifying the Music Classroom

Gamifying the Music Classroom

Digital Tools for Practical Application

ANDREW J. LESSER

Oxford University Press is a department of the University of Oxford. It furthers
the University's objective of excellence in research, scholarship, and education
by publishing worldwide. Oxford is a registered trade mark of Oxford University
Press in the UK and certain other countries.

Published in the United States of America by Oxford University Press
198 Madison Avenue, New York, NY 10016, United States of America.

© Oxford University Press 2024

All rights reserved. No part of this publication may be reproduced, stored in
a retrieval system, or transmitted, in any form or by any means, without the
prior permission in writing of Oxford University Press, or as expressly permitted
by law, by license, or under terms agreed with the appropriate reproduction
rights organization. Inquiries concerning reproduction outside the scope of the
above should be sent to the Rights Department, Oxford University Press, at the
address above.

You must not circulate this work in any other form
and you must impose this same condition on any acquirer.

Library of Congress Cataloging-in-Publication Data
Names: Lesser, Andrew J., author.
Title: Gamifying the music classroom : digital tools for practical application / Andrew J. Lesser.
Description: [1.] | New York : Oxford University Press, 2024. |
Includes bibliographical references and index.
Identifiers: LCCN 2024030408 (print) | LCCN 2024030409 (ebook) |
ISBN 9780197696651 (paperback) | ISBN 9780197696644 (hardback) |
ISBN 9780197696668 (epub) | ISBN 9780197696675 | ISBN 9780197696682 |
ISBN 9780197696699
Subjects: LCSH: Music—Instruction and study. | School music—Instruction
and study. | Video games in education. | Video music games.
Classification: LCC MT1.L5756 G36 2024 (print) | LCC MT1.L5756 (ebook) |
DDC 780.7/7—dc23/eng/20240702
LC record available at https://lccn.loc.gov/2024030408
LC ebook record available at https://lccn.loc.gov/2024030409

DOI: 10.1093/oso/9780197696644.001.0001

Contents

List of Figures — vii
About the Companion Website — ix

1. The Power of Play — 1
2. Getting Started — 19
3. Creating Music With Games — 34
4. Performing Music With Games — 62
5. Responding to Music With Games — 86
6. Connecting Musical Concepts With Games — 115
7. Future Directions — 142

Epilogue — 167
Appendix: List of Games — 169
References — 171
Index of List of Games Cited — 181
General Index — 183

Figures

1.1.	Screenshot of Minecraft note blocks.	2
1.2.	Diagram of the flow state.	6
1.3.	Diagram of the SAMR model.	10
1.4.	Diagram of the TPACK model.	11
1.5.	Diagram of the Triple E Model.	12
2.1.	A simulated instrument controller used in Guitar Hero.	22
2.2.	The Oregon Trail by MECC.	24
3.1.	Rhythm Maker by Google.	38
3.2.	Cyber Pattern Player by PBS Kids.	40
3.3.	Song Maker by Google.	42
3.4.	Online Rhythm Composer by Inside the Orchestra.	44
3.5.	Otogarden by Constantino Oliva.	46
3.6.	Compose Your Own Music by Classics for Kids.	48
3.7.	Compose with Us Now by Inside the Orchestra.	50
3.8.	Incredibox by So Far So Good.	53
3.9.	Compose It by New Bedford Symphony Orchestra.	55
3.10.	Mario Paint Composer by unfun Games.	57
3.11.	Minecraft Open Note Block Studio by Open NBS.	60
4.1.	Carmen's World Orchestra by PBS Kids.	65
4.2.	Peg + Cat Music Maker by PBS Kids.	67
4.3.	Slap Track by HoneyDooDat Productions.	69
4.4.	Match the Rhythm by Classics for Kids.	71
4.5.	Rhythm Cat by Melody Cats.	73
4.6.	Piano Dust Buster 2 by JoyTunes.	76
4.7.	Bemuse: Beat Music Sequencer by T. Pangsakulyanont and N. Suktarachan.	78
4.8.	Note Fighter by MythicOwl.	80
4.9.	Vocal Match by Theta Music Trainer.	82
4.10.	Pitchy Ninja by Pitchy Ninja.	84
5.1.	Pinkamusical Garden by PBS Kids.	89
5.2.	Melody Maker by Google.	91
5.3.	Musical Me! by Duck Duck Goose.	93
5.4.	Note Names by Classics for Kids.	95

Figures

5.5.	Flashnote Derby by Luke Bartolomeo.	97
5.6.	Staff Wars by TMI Media, LLC.	99
5.7.	Staff Dungeon by Dr. Musik.	101
5.8.	Instrument Match by Music Teacher's Games.	104
5.9.	Channel Scramble by Theta Music Trainer.	106
5.10.	Band Match by Theta Music Trainer.	108
5.11.	Tonic Finder by Theta Music Trainer.	111
5.12.	Parrot Phrases by Theta Music Trainer.	113
6.1.	Daniel Tiger: Feel the Music by PBS Kids.	118
6.2.	Chrome Music Lab: Kandinsky by Google.	120
6.3.	Spectrogram by Google.	122
6.4.	Paint with Music by Google Arts and Culture.	124
6.5.	Young Person's Guide to the Orchestra by Carnegie Hall.	127
6.6.	Music Maps by Inside the Orchestra.	129
6.7.	Isle of Tune by HappyLander Ltd.	131
6.8.	Beast Box by Ben Mirin and The Cornell Lab.	134
6.9.	Perfect Pitch by The Kennedy Center.	136
6.10.	Songlio by Encore.	138
6.11.	BeepBox by John Nesky.	140
7.1.	Final Fantasy XIV screenshot.	145
7.2.	Lord of the Rings Online screenshot.	146
7.3.	ArcheAge music player screenshot.	147
7.4.	Sea of Thieves screenshot.	148
7.5.	Scratch Jr. screenshot.	150
7.6.	Makey Makey screenshot.	151
7.7.	Blockly Music screenshot.	152
7.8.	Microsoft MakeCode screenshot.	152
7.9.	Spatial Orchestra (TCW, 2019) screenshot.	154
7.10.	Instant Musician by Music Everywhere screenshot.	155
7.11.	Virtuoso VR screenshot.	158
7.12.	Music Inside screenshot.	159
7.13.	Jam Studio VR screenshot.	159
7.14.	Maestro VR screenshot.	160

About the Companion Website

www.oup.com/us/GamifyingtheMusicClassroom

This book features a companion website that provides material that cannot be made available in a book, namely, tutorial videos of each game outlined in the main text. The videos further illustrate the basic gameplay and design of each example. The reader is encouraged to consult this resource in conjunction with Chapters 3–6. Examples available online are indicated in the text with Oxford's symbol ▶.

1
The Power of Play

Prelude

My students can't stop talking about *Minecraft* (Mojang, 2011). They discuss the best ways to build pixelated structures or to interact with other players they'll most likely never meet in person. They dress up like *Minecraft* characters for Halloween and wear *Minecraft* clothing the rest of the year. They purchase downloadable material that features new "skins" (character attire) to various other items of *Minecraft* merchandise, or, more accurately, they have their parents buy it for them. They talk about it so often that I feel I have almost played it vicariously through them.

I hadn't really played *Minecraft* until years after it was originally released, which is ironic considering that, at the time of this writing, I am in my 40s and still avidly play video games. My students know this, as I like to remind them whenever I feel that I am losing my street-cred. I tell them that I've played plenty of video games before, including open-sandbox Massive Multiplayer Online (MMO) games, or computer-generated fictional worlds where the player can travel as they please while interacting with other online players like *Minecraft*.

Interestingly, *Minecraft* offers a unique feature: the ability to create musical content using in-game mechanics. Students can create and arrange their own melodies by manipulating specific kinds of pixelated blocks called "note blocks," which are normally used to build structures and alter the environment (Figure 1.1). Although *Minecraft* is considered a commercial game and is not specifically designed for music education, it can potentially be applied to explore some of the basic elements of composition, such as pitch, melody, rhythm, improvisation, and form (Abrahams, 2018).

Because of video games such as *Minecraft*, I noticed the teaching potential of digital games in the music classroom. Listening to my own students talk on and on about the newest video game craze made me not only reminisce about my childhood experiences playing games like *Super Mario Bros* (Nintendo, 1985) and *The Legend of Zelda* (Nintendo, 1986), but gave me an opportunity to explore how digital games designed for educational purposes could enhance my ability to teach music more effectively. Sharing my enjoyment of video games with my students has also given me the opportunity to build positive rapport on a personal and relatable level, something that has become increasingly essential in today's educational environment.

Since technology has become not only an indispensable, but mandated, requirement in the modern public-school curriculum, it makes sense that the digital tools that we employ should be enjoyable and related to students' interests. Video games have grown to be a major source of home entertainment, with 65% of American

Figure 1.1. Screenshot of *Minecraft* note blocks. Public domain.

households in 2023 containing at least one video game player (ESA, 2023). This accounts for approximately 212.6 million individuals who enjoy gaming on a regular basis, 76% of whom are under the age of 18. Even more striking are the 62% of adults who play, many of whom do so not only for entertainment, but also to feel connected with others and to explore realms of the imagination that may not be present in any other form of recreation.

These facts have not been lost among educators, as games "modded" (modified) and created for teaching purposes have been in use since the 1970s. In my own childhood experiences, my parents saw the potential of how games could be harnessed for learning by purchasing educationally based games such as *The Oregon Trail* (MECC, 1974), *Reader Rabbit* (The Learning Company, 1983), and *Math Blaster* (Davidson & Associates, 1983) to supplement my school studies. This strategy was seemingly successful not just with my generation, as these games are still available online and have gone through several upgraded versions. Even *Minecraft*, which was originally designed for purely entertainment purposes, has been modified to help teach academic subjects such as physics, geography, history, and math (Sáez-López, Miller, Vásquez-Cano, & Garrido, 2015).

Explorations into game-based learning and gamification have been going on for many decades now, but the subcategory of digital game-based learning, those strictly focused on video games, is still relatively in its infancy. Even more so, scholarly works on video games in education have been centered mostly on academic subjects such as language arts, math, science, and social studies, which is ironic considering that video game design requires no small amount of artistic creativity. Music education is no stranger to computer game-based instruction, having been using digital technology since the 1960s (Kuhn & Allvin, 1967; Webster, 2002). However, with more music teachers now having grown up with technology as opposed to their predecessors, their innate understanding and experience with video games has led to the rapid growth of digital resources as tools for music learning.

Prensky (2001, 2006) referred to this generational gap as the difference between "digital immigrants" and "digital natives." Digital immigrants are those who were raised before the introduction of specific technologies and have had to adapt accordingly, while digital natives were born with this technology already established and thus are much more comfortable with using it. I, for example, was born before the advent of the internet, cell phones, CDs, and social media. I didn't take my first formal computer class until I was a junior in high school, and in many cases, I still feel that I must keep up with the ever-changing technological landscape. However, knowledge of this medium is not only recommended for effective educators, but also is now required to understand the world of our digitally native students.

As younger teachers continue to enter the educational field, it is likely to assume that their familiarity with technology will result in a much greater application in their teaching practices (Bensiger, 2012; Kersten, 2006). Since the 1970s, video games have become a major part of both children's and adult culture, and teachers who were brought up with the popularity of video games would therefore be more likely to view and use them as educational tools. However, using digital games to enhance music instruction can be adapted by all teachers who have an interest and willingness to add these tools to their practice.

How to Use This Book

This text is not only designed to advance the concept that digital game-based instruction can be effective as a tool to help teach and reinforce musical concepts and skills, but also to provide practical applications that will assist any preservice or practicing music educator who is either in the process of building a music program or working to enhance an already existing one. To accomplish this use, we will discuss how video games can improve knowledge-based structures, engagement, meaningful experiences, and social-emotional learning. We will also explore how they can impact students' abilities in musical contexts and how we as teachers can relate them to National Core Arts Standards in detailed lesson plans that can be used in classroom settings with varying technology availability.

With that said, it is important to remember that video games in and of themselves are simply a tool in the proverbial toolbox; they are not a singular material to be used in all examples of teaching. I use a variety of methodologies, including performance practice, close reading, composition by hand, and other activities besides video games in my curriculum. While video games are some of my favorite materials to use in the classroom, I make sure that I am not limited to my approaches just for the sake of using popular technology.

As such, readers may study the entire book as a whole or peruse sections of it as they believe it applies to them. This text does not have to be read in sequence to be effective for those who are looking for a specific concept they wish to reinforce or a particular area on which they should focus. Feel free to jump to any section that suits your interest and read the sections in any order you choose. One of the most enjoyable features of many of today's video games is the ability they give players to freely explore exciting and fantastical worlds without always having to immediately follow the predetermined path. This ability gives them the opportunity to absorb and enjoy the experience at their own pace without the fear and embarrassment of making a mistake. I believe that teaching music should operate under the same construct.

Why Digital Games?

When compared to other forms of multimedia, digital games may have a distinct advantage in the way that they can engage and hold a player's attention through a degree of interactivity that may not be present in other formats (; Smuts, 2009). Video games can provide activities and tasks that engage players intellectually and challenge their thinking through active game elements and that can command the attention of the player through meaningful objectives. Video games transform an individual from a passive recipient into an active participant; they transform content from abstract concepts to tools that the learner can use to accomplish specific goals; and they transform the context of learning into a reality that is immediately relevant to a person's actions (Barab, Gresalfi, & Arici, 2009). By playing video games, previous paradigms of interactivity can be enhanced through developing critical thinking skills, creating meaningful experiences, and converting enjoyment into the acquisition of knowledge.

Cognitive Development

The act of playing to increase knowledge, solve problems, and improve sensory processes was studied long before the popularity of video games entered the educational field. Piaget (1962) saw playing games as an opportunity for development of the imagination, especially in young children. While children are learning the rules and norms of their respective cultures, they are also creating imaginary worlds without limitations. Playing allows children to fully immerse themselves in these worlds freely without the fear of consequences or feelings of shame and embarrassment. Similarly, Vygotsky (1978) saw play as a leading factor of child development in that it facilitates interactions between the child and their environment, which can help to solve problems that arise from the realization of the child's developing mind.

The use of digital games as cognitive tools can make the student an active participant in their own educational processes, which include collaboration, creativity, and innovative problem solving (Gee, 2003; Squire, 2011). Effective digital games for educational practice therefore involve specific features inherent to the design of the program not only to achieve these goals, but to simultaneously engage and motivate the players to invest themselves in their educational development. Digital games can serve as vehicles for declarative knowledge (factual ideas), conceptual knowledge (grouping of similar thoughts and ideas), structure-based knowledge (rules and relationships), procedural knowledge (performing a specific task or tasks), and psychomotor development (Kapp, 2012).

Relatively few connections have been made between digital game-based learning and music education, but an increasing amount of research is being conducted that supports the theory that video games can have a positive impact on developing cognitive ability in musical contexts (Austin, 2016; Benedict & O'Leary, 2019; Gower & McDowell, 2012; Lesser, 2020; Paney & Kay, 2014; Richardson & Kim, 2011; Tobias, 2012; Tobias & O'Leary, 2016). These studies, among others, contribute evidence to the learning possibilities of video games and how music educators can benefit from their inclusion in the classroom.

Personal Relevance

The theory of video games as an effective supplement to education due to their relation to personal experience can be linked to the philosophy of progressivism as conceived by John Dewey. Unfortunately, Dewey himself was not able to see the development and impact of the video game industry, but researchers of digital game-based learning believe that he would have approved of the innovations that video games have brought to education (Shaffer, 2006; Squire, 2011; Waddington, 2015).

In *Experience and Education*, Dewey proposed that basing education on personal experience would result in a more meaningful connection between the student and the subject matter (Dewey, 1938). Additionally, creating a shared participatory experience that can be organized where all participants have something valuable to contribute can be worthwhile when linked to a curriculum (McDermott, 1981). The multitudes of video games that can be played cooperatively and competitively require habits of strategic inquiry and knowledge of social interactions that can be easily applied to real-world relationships (Waddington, 2015).

To say that video games have made a major impact on our collective societal and cultural consciousness is an understatement; the Entertainment Software Association estimated in 2023 that nearly 212.6 million Americans play video games (Entertainment Software Association, 2023). According to the report, 86% of players agree that video games bring joy through play. Games can inspire, provide mental stimulation, offer opportunities for collaboration, and relieve stress. Families also play digital games together: 76% of parents played video games with their children at least weekly.

During the Covid-19 pandemic, 55% of players stated that they played more games, and 90% of players reported that they would continue playing after social distancing was no longer required. In addition, 71% of parents saw video games as an effective source of stress relief for their children, 59% of parents said their children also used educational games, and 66% of parents said video games made their children's transition to remote learning easier. When used effectively, digital games can be adapted for educational practices by combining experiential learning, purposeful knowledge, and user enjoyment.

Engagement and Motivation

The primary factor explaining why playing video games is so culturally influential is not necessarily its potential for psychological and cognitive development, but the fact that the act of play, specifically playing games, can elicit a deep sense of fun (Koster, 2014). Fostering motivation and engagement through both playing music and playing video games can be explored using the constructs of self-determination theory. Self-determination theory, as defined by Ryan, Rigby, and Przybylski (2006), is a theory of how intrinsic and extrinsic motivation is affected by psychological causes such as the need for autonomy, proficiency, and a sense of purpose.

Self-determination theory emphasizes that motivation results from the ability to pursue activities independently, the desire to increase in skill, and a strong relevance to personal interests (Pink, 2009; Rigby & Ryan, 2011). Playing music and playing video games can both be associated with these changes in well-being, provided that the act of playing is engaging enough for the player that they experience not only enjoyment, but also a sense of fulfillment in performing that activity that they continue for lengthy periods of time.

The enjoyment, immersion, and engagement of both music and video games can lead to the phenomenon of what psychologist Mihalyi Csikszentmihalyi described as a "flow state" (Csikszentmihalyi, 1975a; 1975b; 1990). According to Csikszentmihalyi, a flow state is achieved when "people are so involved in an activity that nothing else seems to matter; the experience itself is so enjoyable that people will do it at great cost, for the sheer sake of doing it" (1990, 4).

An activity meets the criteria for the flow state when the level of challenge presented by the activity itself slightly exceeds the participant's skill level (Figure 1.2). When the individual is participating in the activity, it creates a deep state of enjoyment and satisfaction that time itself seems to slow down and everything outside of the activity fades away. However, if the activity presents itself as too little of

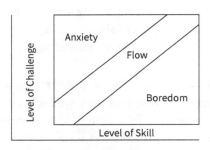

Figure 1.2. Diagram of the flow state (adapted from Csikszentmihalyi, 1990)

a challenge, the participant will experience boredom and will not reach a flow state. Conversely, if the challenge is too difficult for the participant to handle, then the anxiety created by not being able to effectively keep up will also reduce the potential of reaching a flow state.

However, players who constantly practice and improve their skills with these games and others will eventually increase their proficiency, resulting in a greater opportunity to experience a flow state. The parallels between this phenomenon and the act of playing music are apparent, particularly when comparing the process of learning each activity. Just like learning musical skills, a video game player must develop and practice specific skills to successfully complete in-game tasks and objectives. This may be challenging at first, but with time, dedication, and hard work the player will eventually become proficient. The experience that practicing music and playing video games both contain is what Lazzaro (2004) referred to as "hard fun," or a deep enjoyment that only comes with prevailing over a difficult task.

Scaffolding

Because students possess varying ability levels, teachers must develop differential methods of support as they learn new skills. Many digital games provide customizable difficulty settings to give an appropriate amount of challenge. As the player's skills begin to improve, they may wish to increase the amount of challenge by moving to the next level. Games that are designed for educational purposes may possess an advantage in the fact that players would normally have a teacher that can instruct them as to the game's mechanics and assist them if they are having difficulty. Games can also inherently provide the scaffolding needed for players to successfully complete tasks as they grow more difficult, difficulty that gradually decreases as the player becomes more proficient (Rooney, 2012; Vygotsky, 1978).

These skills can be developed with assistance from teachers through which the ability level of the player reaches the level of potential skill. Vygotsky (1978) referred to this as a "zone of proximal development" (102), where the demand of problem solving forces the individual to create new and innovative solutions using creative thinking. The zone of proximal development is the space between the student's actual developmental level and the level they can achieve with the assistance of a teacher. Learning to play both music and games can act as a zone of proximal development, where the player's set skill level and potential ability are bridged with instructional guidance.

Gee (2003) described this phenomenon as a "regime of competence," whereby exploration and experimentation with multiple pathways to success are usually rewarded. In addition, failure is not punished with permanent consequences, and multiple attempts are permitted, allowing the player to learn from their mistakes and develop more effective strategies to succeed. This is also known throughout the gaming community as "Bushnell's Law," named after Atari founder Nolan

Bushnell and states that effective games should be easy to learn but difficult to master (Ibrahim, Vela, Rodríguiez, Sánchez, & Zea, 2012).

The feedback received from the game's construct can contribute to the overall assessment and evaluation of the student's ability. Effective educational game design naturally embeds these assessments into the learning process while maintaining the player's engagement level. This process has been referred to as "stealth assessment" (Shute, 2011), which has the added benefit of reducing the anxiety commonly associated with taking tests or other benchmarks. The ultimate goal is to eliminate the difference between active learning and skill evaluation, allowing for simultaneous practice and assessment through active play.

Social-Emotional Learning

One of the main reasons why gaming and music are effective means of prosocial development is due to the intense feelings of gratification they elicit through consistent participation. Playing music and playing games can create positive feelings of accomplishment and satisfaction, which has the additional effect of building confidence, accepting failure, and learning delayed gratification (Ryan et al., 2006). Adapting to negative emotional experiences such as frustration and anxiety, can help strengthen emotional regulation and allow the participant to be better prepared for hardships that occur in everyday social situations. This ability is crucial in developing a positive identity that is centered on self-esteem, emotional growth, and social skills.

Developing a prosocial personal identity is largely influenced by the social groups in which we associate (Grooten & Kowert, 2015). Musicians frequently socialize with other musicians in both professional and personal environments because of the feeling of belonging with people who have similar perspectives. Not only does this give the individual ownership of the identity that represents their character, but it serves as a connection to others who share the same interests to the point where it becomes an essential part of a positive self-image. The same can be said of other pursuits that become so important to an individual that they define themselves by their involvement in that activity, including sports, academics, hobbies, and other sources of personal significance.

Likewise, those who play video games can also build positive self-identities through interactions with other gamers. Collaborative games, commonly referred to as MMORPG's (Massive Multiplayer Online Role-Playing Games), are communities of large groups of players that represent various nationalities, gender identifications, religions, creeds, ages, races, and other demographics, working together to achieve in-game tasks and objectives. Cooperative play can help foster skills such as making quick decisions, strategizing, taking risks, and developing leadership. This is most often experienced in the form of a collaborative effort where the participants are vying to achieve a shared goal.

Video games that feature musical creation and performance as either a core element or side activity have resulted in online collaborations that produce a unique form of self-expression. These social communities, or "sonic participatory cultures" (O'Leary & Tobias, 2016), allow users to create, perform, and share music in real time with games that foster virtual communities such as *Minecraft*, *The Lord of the Rings Online* (Turbine, 2007), and the *Guitar Hero/Rock Band* (Harmonix, 2005, 2008) series, among others (Cheng, 2014; Miller, 2012). The educational industry has made use of online platforms to collaborate and interact, such as Google Classroom, Canvas, Blackboard, and Moodle. As more educators experiment with online sharing as a source of musical networking, the opportunities for students to engage and work with others can result in a much greater sense of belonging with those who feel the same passion.

Digital Games in the Music Curriculum

Applying technology in music education is by no means a recent concept. Digital programs used to supplement instruction have been integrated into nearly every type of music learning environment for several decades. A plethora of resources ranging from digital audio workstations (DAWs), notation software, online practice and recording programs, websites, and other applications are available to all music educators who possess the necessary equipment. Learning to manipulate technology appropriately has become a cornerstone of educational best practices to support what is now referred to as digital citizenship and twenty-first-century skills (International Society for Technology in Education, 2022).

Though digital game-based learning has been increasingly successful in gaining acceptance within the educational community, it remains important to consider how games can be used in the context of effective teaching. Digital games, like any other examples of technology, are ultimately just materials that can be beneficial or detrimental to students based on their usage. To this end, several models describing how technology can be successfully incorporated into the classroom were developed to assist educators in connecting to specific content areas. The guidelines presented in these models can not only serve as a framework for measuring if using digital games are indeed fostering learning, but as a justification for acquiring support from school administrators and the general community.

The SAMR Model

Developed by Dr. Ruben R. Puentedura in 2010, the SAMR model consists of four tiers of technology integration: Substitution, Augmentation, Modification, and Redefinition (Terada, 2020). Substitution (Figure 1.3) involves changing traditional materials such as paper documents with digital materials. This stage is becoming

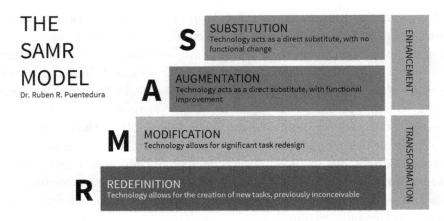

Figure 1.3. Diagram of the SAMR model. Image retrieved from Youki Terada, "A Powerful Model for Understanding Good Tech Integration," *Edutopia*, May 4, 2020, https://www.edutopia.org/article/powerful-model-understanding-good-tech-integration. Available under a Creative Commons License.

more common in music classrooms, where working with composition programs such as notation generators and sequencing software has largely replaced working with pencils and manuscript paper. Other examples include substituting flashcards, worksheets, and assessments with online game-based tools such as Quizlet, Yousician, and Kahoot.

Augmentation, like substitution, also incorporates digital enhancements such as websites, multimedia, software programs, and social media to increase student efficiency and engagement. For example, virtual online instruments that students can play using a portable media device may be more cost-effective than purchasing an entire set of instruments. The Substitution and Augmentation stages act as enrichments where the general content of the learning task is largely unchanged, while the next two stages transform the activity where technology becomes an integral part of generating educational outcomes.

The Modification phase features technology materials as a core element of a lesson or unit. Using online tools such as Google Classroom, Canvas, or Moodle can transform a traditional learning environment into a more interactive platform for communicating and sharing student output. Digital games that are designed to train and assess musical skills can function as independent activities that can enhance student learning by providing meaningful and immediate feedback.

Finally, the Redefinition phase facilitates instruction in ways that would not have been possible without the use of technological resources. To this end, entire digital curricula such as Quaver, MusicEDU, and MusicFirst have been introduced to music educators as comprehensive teaching aids that provide lesson materials, assessments, and student progress monitors. Digital game-based learning on this level can provide frameworks for independent practice through formal assessment, in addition to communication and collaboration among students that allow for the exploration of previously inaccessible knowledge domains and learner capabilities (Puentedura, 2021).

The TPACK Model

TPACK stands for Technological Pedagogical Content Knowledge, which was coined by researchers Punya Mishra and Matthew Koehler in 2006. The TPACK framework creates bridges between three aspects of knowledge: knowledge of technology, knowledge of learning content, and pedagogical knowledge (Mishra & Koehler, 2006). The three knowledge bases form seven components that create different combinations of skill domains, such as Pedagogical Content Knowledge (PCK), or knowing musical content and effective teaching practices, but not how to integrate technology to help reach learning objectives (Figure 1.4). Likewise, having a thorough grounding in technological resources and content knowledge will be ineffective in educational environments if the teacher does not possess the necessary pedagogical knowledge Technical Content Knowledge (TCK).

The goal of TPACK is to build expertise in all three areas of knowledge to maximize the connection between content, pedagogy, and the use of technology. Reaching this

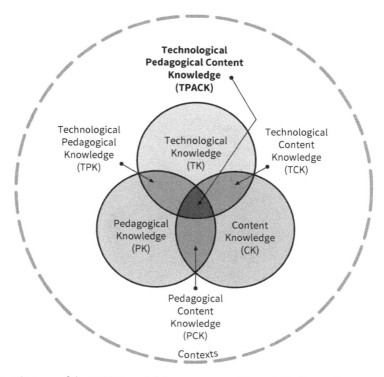

Figure 1.4. Diagram of the TPACK model. Image retrieved from http://www.tpack.org/. Reproduced by permission of the publisher, © 2012 by tpack.org.

goal requires an understanding of the representation of concepts using technology, pedagogical techniques that use technology, and knowledge of how technology can help develop new pathways of learning (Koehler, 2012). As reflected in the TPACK model, digital game-based learning is at its most effective when the teacher is experienced not only in playing the selected games, but also in integrating those games to reach educational objectives. This learning is further enhanced when the games are already rooted in thematic content that involves building musical skills and knowledge.

The Triple E Model

The Triple E Model, as shared with SAMR and TPACK, measures the degree to which technology is assisting students in meeting predesigned educational objectives (Kolb, 2020). The framework for this model was designed in 2011 by Liz Kolb as a coaching tool to support teachers in selecting technology tools that combine with effective instructional strategies. The three "E's" of the model represent Engagement, Enhancement, and Extension (Figure 1.5). Each aspect relates to each other to create a feedback loop that informs and affects how technology is integrated into learning goals.

The essential questions that are devoted to each "E" should be asked before implementing any digital game into a classroom environment. Gamification is designed to promote engagement and motivation through actively involving students in ways that transcend traditional instructional methods (i.e., lecture, skill-and-drill). However, using digital games for the sake of simply getting students to

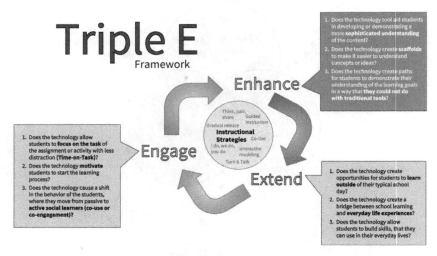

Figure 1.5. Diagram of the Triple E Model. Image retrieved from https://www.tripleeframework.com/framework-models.html. Available under a Creative Commons Attribution-NonCommercial 4.0 International License https://creativecommons.org/licenses/by-nc/4.0.

become more interested in the material does not necessarily make them an effective learning tool. The games must also promote a deeper understanding of the content in a way that may not have been possible with other methods of instruction. This is particularly important during the selection process, specifically in answering the question of not only if the gaming tool is relevant to the learning task, but if playing the game creates a connection between music and their everyday lives. All three frameworks promote the use of technology such as digital games to support music learning, but it is the teacher's decisions of what games to use and how to use them that will largely affect their success in the classroom.

Digital Games and Core Arts Standards

One of the most important elements when designing lessons to fit into a music curriculum is how they can be related to overarching learning standards. These standards help reinforce accountability and are generally required to be incorporated into every lesson, regardless of the subject or grade level. The College Board for the National Coalition for Core Arts Standards compared Arts Education Standards in 13 countries and found similarities in areas such as cultural understanding, critical and creative thinking, problem solving, communication, and fostering a sense of well-being (The College Board, 2013). These standards are closely related to the American National Core Arts Standards, namely, Creating, Performing, Responding, and Connecting. Each process branches into several anchor standards and establishes the context for an overarching representation of music literacy.

Creating: Conceiving and developing new artistic ideas and work

- Anchor Standard #1: Generate and conceptualize new artistic ideas and work.
- Anchor Standard #2: Organize and develop artistic ideas and work.
- Anchor Standard #3: Refine and complete artistic work.

Digital games that involve the creation of original artistic work are not normally considered games as traditionally defined, that is, as being situated in a competitive environment wherein exists the possibility of winning or losing (Salen & Zimmerman, 2004). However, the addition of game-based elements such as incorporating characters, immersive graphics, and unlockable bonuses after completing a specific task can engage a user in ways that traditional DAWs and other composition programs may not.

Commercial games have experimented with this design as mini games not required to complete the game, but as fun diversions that players can spend time generating and sharing original work. In addition to the note block musical composition feature within *Minecraft*, games such as *Little Big Planet 3* (Sony Computer Entertainment, 2014) and *Animal Crossing: New Horizons* (Nintendo, 2020) contain in-game music generators that are not part of the main game and can be used freely without fear of failing an objective. Since these games require use of a dedicated console, games that focus on the Creating standard which are more accessible and cost-effective will be discussed in Chapter 3.

Performing: Realizing artistic ideas and work through interpretation and presentation.

- Anchor Standard #4: Select, analyze, and interpret artistic work for presentation.
- Anchor Standard #5: Develop and refine artistic techniques and work for presentation.
- Anchor Standard #6: Convey meaning through the presentation of artistic work.

Performing is at the heart of playing digital games; the player must manipulate in-game events to accomplish tasks and objectives to complete the game. This involves employing strategies that the player has learned by progressing through the game and practicing new skills. Performing music is very similar to this method, which game designers have recognized with the creation of the music performance genre, defined by games such as *Guitar Hero* (Harmonix, 2005) and *Rock Band* (Harmonix, 2008).

An entire litany of games that conform to the *Guitar Hero* formula have been developed with various themes, gameplay features, and musical examples. These games, however, are primarily designed for entertainment purposes, and any development of musical skills is largely unintentional and learned as a by-product. Regardless, these games have enjoyed enduring popularity and continue to be influential in the video game industry. Practicing musical performance skills has also been explored through digital games that can be used in conjunction with musical instruments or the player's voice. Games that are designed for these specific purposes are illustrated in Chapter 4.

Responding: Understanding and evaluating how the arts convey meaning.

- Anchor Standard #7: Perceive and analyze artistic work.
- Anchor Standard #8: Interpret intent and meaning in artistic work.
- Anchor Standard #9: Apply criteria to evaluate artistic work.

Responding to musical prompts requires knowledge of musical concepts and terminology to fully perceive and understand how specific works of music convey meaning. This entails identifying the basic elements of music, such as pitch, rhythm, tempo, dynamics, and other concepts that musicians use to describe and evaluate musical work. Building musical skills to fully appreciate and interpret examples of music can only be accomplished through dedicated study and practice of these individual musical fundamentals.

Digital games can provide educators with an effective tool to train these concepts in an engaging setting that alleviates the potential boredom of traditional skill-and-drill activities. While many games do still rely on quiz-based formats, the use of additional components such as a competitive interface along with a rewards system grounded in immediate feedback can enhance the learning experience. Games that assist in the acquisition of musical concepts and skills will be highlighted in Chapter 5.

Connecting: Relating artistic ideas and work with personal meaning and external context.

- Anchor Standard #10: Synthesize and relate knowledge and personal experiences to make art.
- Anchor Standard #11: Relate artistic ideas and works with societal, cultural, and historical context to deepen understanding.

The role of the Connecting standard is to derive meaning from musical experiences not only in a personal context, but in relation to a global understanding that builds tolerance and respect for diversity. This is represented not only in terms of different cultures, but also race, gender, and historical significance. Commercial games have delved into these societal aspects since their inception, though they have not always been accurate in their portrayals. Educational games, known commonly as "edutainment," strive to provide correct information while attempting to create the engagement that commercial games possess.

Games that connect arts education with related subjects can be compared to the objectives of STEM (Science, Technology, Engineering, and Math). Successful efforts to expand the concept of STEM to inherently include the arts, or STEAM, can be heightened by including digital games that combine these elements. Additionally, digital games can be used in context with not only musical content but including other aspects of the arts as well. Games that promote connections between music and these other disciplines will be presented in Chapter 6.

Linking Games to Pedagogical Approaches

Educational philosophy as applied to music has taken the form of several systematic approaches to classroom music learning. Each unique approach is dedicated to the goal of providing the optimal methodology of building musical skills and knowledge; yet the procedure of disseminating this knowledge varies between styles. Many music teachers have identified with a particular style and teach exclusively using that pedagogical approach, while other teachers may practice none or a combination of these philosophies. In many cases, interconnections can be found between these methods; including digital games as part of a curriculum that is designed around one or more established pedagogies is a natural extension of the possibilities available to music teachers.

Orff Schulwerk

The Orff teaching methodology began in Germany due to composer and educator Carl Orff's (1895–1982) interest in combining music, theater, and dance employing instruments that students could use to create and improvise their own music. These instruments, designed as primarily rhythmic barred percussion, included scaled-down xylophones, marimbas, and glockenspiels to move away from traditional piano training that had been part of the physical education curriculum (Benedict, 2010). In addition, string and woodwind instruments such as the cello and recorder were gradually incorporated to add long drone sounds to the harmonic texture.

Metallophone instruments and body percussion complement the developing singing voice that is fostered through folk songs, nursery rhymes, and singing games. Movement is also a large part of the Orff process and consists of natural play activities such as jumping, skipping, spinning, and running. Games are of particular importance as Orff teaching is based on the concept that active participation encourages students to experience and internalize music on their developmental level. Orff teaching embraces the idea of using digital games and other multimedia as tools for student engagement and creativity, and numerous resources are available online to explore these possibilities (Burns, 2020).

Kodály Method

Zoltán Kodály (1882–1967) dedicated his career as a composer and teacher to the advancement of music education in his native Hungary. Kodály collected and analyzed hundreds of Hungarian folk songs to emphasize singing as the fundamental musical experience. Expanding upon Kodály's philosophy, Patterson (2020) noted that music representing a nation's unique culture can be highly influential in teaching the foundations of music. In addition to folk songs, practitioners of the Kodály method sing traditional children's songs and games that involve movement and specific actions.

Although Kodály initially envisioned appropriate musical repertoire as folk songs that had been embedded into Hungarian cultural traditions, this perspective does not exclude more recent popular songs that have a cultural effect on today's society. Modern researchers of music learning theory, such as Edwin Gordon, Shinichi Suzuki, and John Feierabend, owe much of their individual methodologies to Kodály's work, particularly in the use of songs inherent to a child's culture as a foundation for music literacy (Strong, 2020). Popular songs spanning multiple genres have an immense sphere of influence and are more commonly available through media technology (Roulston, 2002). Media have also played an increased role in children's prior musical experiences and how they are using digital technologies. Digital games that use any form of music that reflects popular culture can be incorporated into the

Kodály approach, if the objective of using such games corresponds to established National Core Arts Standards.

Dalcroze Eurhythmics

Rhythmic movement, along with ear training, improvisation, and solfege, are the defining processes for Émile Jaques-Dalcroze's (1865–1950) approach to music development. The Dalcroze method is designed for creating a strong sense of performance through rhythm and body awareness in a playful manner that can be applied to people of all ages (Dalcroze Society of America, 2022). The relationship between physical movement and space, known as kinesthesia, creates a sensory intuitiveness to music education that combines with musical concepts to produce potentially greater mental acuity (Anderson, 2011).

Digital games can create a natural connection to the Dalcroze method in the way that it requires physical movement to manipulate tasks through an external interface (Nijs, 2018). Creative programs that use game-based learning with technology such as touchscreens, controllers, and cameras can transform passive learners into active participants. This effect is present in many commercial games that use movement as the core element of gameplay, including *Dance Dance Revolution* (Konami, 1998) and *Just Dance* (Ubisoft, 2009), among many others. These games encourage refined motor skills by developing the ability to synchronize and maintain a steady beat, reproduce and perform symbolically notated rhythms, and improve sight-reading ability through basic rhythmic shapes (Auerbach, 2010).

Unfortunately, commercially available dance-based music video games require a dedicated console to play and only allow one or a small group to play at a time. However, online versions of this gaming genre are becoming available for portable devices with built-in camera capability. *Just Dance Now* (Ubisoft, 2014), for example, is available for free on smartphones, and more versions of games previously only available on consoles are being released for computers, laptops, and virtual reality headsets.

Summary

In this chapter, we discussed how digital games can reinforce and enhance the experience of learning and practicing music. Studies in digital game-based learning have been conducted by researchers and game enthusiasts for several decades, but its applications to music education are still relatively in its infancy. Regardless, digital games have the potential to assist educational practices in the context of cognitive learning, personal relevance, engagement and motivation, scaffolding, social-emotional learning, and building identities.

Models that outline effective methods of integrating technology into a music curriculum, such as SAMR, TPACK, and Triple E, can also involve the inclusion of digital games as additional tools, if they are used in collaboration with educational objectives as presented in Core Arts Standards frameworks. Each of these standards, which primarily include Creating, Performing, Responding, and Connecting, is featured with specific games in detailed lesson plans throughout Chapters 3–6. Music educators that subscribe to established pedagogies, such as Orff, Kodály, and Dalcroze, may also benefit from adding digital game-based materials to their teaching practices.

Chapter 2 will examine the multiple ways in which digital game-based learning can be applied in the classroom, ranging from commercial games to those games designed solely for educational purposes. This will also include the organization of implementing games, from technical specifications to environmental and financial considerations. Additionally, strategies for troubleshooting issues such as technical difficulties and navigating controversies will be featured to facilitate an easier transition for those with less experience with this form of technology.

2
Getting Started

Prelude

When I first began teaching, the widespread use of technology in education was still relatively new. Materials like Smart Boards, Smart Panels, iPads, laptops, online classroom platforms, and educator forums were considered emerging innovations and were not yet mandated as teaching tools. I grew up in the 1980s, and so my first computer was an Apple IIc, which was only good for writing papers and playing *Pac-Man*. I didn't take my first formal computer class until I was a junior in high school, and I didn't have my first cell phone (not to be confused with a Smartphone) until I was in my 20s.

According to Prensky (2001), I would be considered a digital immigrant, someone who did not grow up with this kind of technology and had to adapt. Children can now use iPhones and tablets before they go to kindergarten, and they have a greater understanding of how to manipulate technology than any prior generation. Keeping up with the latest developments and upgrades is difficult enough, let alone being able to implement them in a classroom environment. This is also highly determined by a school's budgetary resources and the ability to obtain, install, and service complex equipment. A teacher could be functioning in a situation with one computer with a projection device, several computer or portable devices, or an available device for each individual student.

Even remote or hybrid learning, which was hardly considered a viable form of instruction prior to 2020, has become commonplace in school districts. To account for the lack of available technology among all students, districts provided laptops, Chromebooks, and other portable internet-capable hardware so that all students could equally participate in online classes. Many districts continued to provide laptops to students after in-person learning was reestablished for use both in the classroom and at home.

As online tools became more frequently used both in remote and in-person classroom environments, technology developers began accelerating their output of educational digital tools as web-based services. These services included game-based applications, though the application of games designed for education had already been in use since the 1970s. This chapter begins by addressing the forms of games as determined by their objectives, whether they be solely for entertainment purposes or for learning practice.

We will then discuss how to establish digital games as a tool for learning, which depends largely on what equipment is available to the teacher. Teachers usually operate in one of four situations: a 1:1 device class, where each individual student has access to a digital device; a 1: multiple device class, where a few devices are available, but not enough for all students to use simultaneously; a 1 device class, which usually consists of a teacher-controlled Smart Board or Smart Panel; and a remote environment, where everyone is streaming the class online from their own home computers or devices.

Each of these four situations can be adapted for use in digital game-based learning, depending on the type of game used and how well it fits into the learning objective or objectives. I have had the opportunity to work in all four environments, using available devices such as iPads, laptops, Chromebooks, a Smartboard, a Smart Panel, and of course, teaching remotely. This merits a discussion on how each piece of equipment can be used independently or in combination to provide an effective experience that can be shared equally by all students.

Finally, we will examine the potential hindrances of using video games in the classroom, including dealing with technical issues, navigating controversies, and gaining support from essential stakeholders such as administration and the general community. While digital game-based learning has made large strides over the past several years in establishing a mainstream following among educators, many teachers are still hesitant to use this resource because of a lack of perceived ability or knowledge of how to incorporate them into an existing curriculum.

While every logistical situation may be different depending on a number of factors, including finances, demographics, time available, and administrative support, educators can incorporate digital games in a variety of ways using the resources they already possess. This chapter will serve to help organize these resources in a way that is well suited to each individual setup. We begin by comparing different types of video games, their advantages and disadvantages, along with an analysis of their feasibility for implementation in the music classroom.

COTS and Edutainment Games

The word "gamification" is a relatively vague term that has only become present in the educational lexicon in the last few decades (Deterding, Dixon, Khaled, & Nacke, 2011; Kapp, 2012). While game-based learning researchers may disagree as to its origin, their main consensus is that it serves two different methodologies of how games are incorporated into learning objectives. First, it can refer to the act of including a topic that would not initially be introduced in a gaming format but modifying the lesson to present it using a game-based structure. For example, a teacher could take the subject of instrument families and create a "Jeopardy"-style game where students could be divided into teams and compete against each other for an incentive.

Game-based learning can also be defined by using materials that already represent a gaming format, incorporating them into the lesson to introduce the topic, reinforce practice, or measure assessment. Games that do not have any direct relation to the lesson material may be modified to suit the purposes of the learning objective, such as using board games like Monopoly to help teach financial literacy and mathematics. Games that offer features like establishing clear goals, instant feedback, a quantitative scoring system, competition and collaboration, social engagement, the freedom to fail without consequences, and embedded rewards all lend themselves well to adaptation to different topics (Dicheva, Dichev, Agre, & Angelova, 2015).

In order to integrate previously published games into a lesson plan, teachers need to fit the game into the context of the objective, which would include being familiar with the game's rules and mechanics and how to assess student knowledge (Young et al., 2012). To that end, many games have been designed to meet various educational objectives in a wide range of topics. These games, commonly known as "edutainment," attempt to blend the commercial value of those designed for entertainment purposes with learning objectives that help foster engagement and motivation among students.

Another type of game that pushes the boundaries of what would be considered traditional is exploration games, or games that have no competitive element. These games rely on player exploration through narrative to create a multimedia interactive experience where the player does not have to be concerned with failing. Though this may not necessarily be considered as part of what defines a true game, such as competition and a quantitative scoring system, many games reflecting this format have become popular in both commercial and educational markets, such as *Dear Esther* (The Chinese Room, 2012), *Firewatch* (Campo Santo, 2016), and *What Remains of Edith Finch* (Giant Sparrow, 2017). Each gaming framework offers opportunities for teachers to present and reinforce musical concepts and skills, and each presents different advantages and drawbacks that must be considered before deciding to use a specific game in a lesson.

Commercial Games

Commercial-off-the-shelf, or COTS games, are games designed solely for entertainment purposes and advertised to a wide demographic to increase marketability. Music in COTS games has been used in a variety of ways, from background ambience to a central element of the core gameplay. The latter, known as rhythm-action games, typically have similar gameplay features in which the player must use rhythmic awareness and motor skills to progress using simulations of musical instruments and/or physical motions. Inputs can be as simple as pressing combinations of buttons on a standard controller or more complicated by using a specific interface, such as a guitar-shaped controller in *Guitar Hero* (Figure 2.1).

The first COTS games dedicated to replicating musical rhythm by movement were created as an early effort for video games to cross over into the fitness industry. *Dance Aerobics* (Human Entertainment, 1989) used a peripheral accessory known as the Power Pad, where players would place their feet or hands on specific pads in

Figure 2.1. A simulated instrument controller used in *Guitar Hero*. Public domain via Wikimedia Commons.

time with the on-screen rhythmic prompts. In addition to the main game, *Dance Aerobics* also included a mode where players could create melodies by stepping on different pads, which played a variety of pitches. This would be followed by a plethora of movement-based rhythm games, including *Dance Dance Revolution* (Konami, 1998), *Just Dance* (Ubisoft, 2009), *Fantasia: Music Evolved* (Harmonix, 2014), and *Beat Saber* (Beat Games, 2019).

The medium that players use to interact with musical prompts can range from traditional gaming controllers to hardware that resembles musical instruments. This hardware includes simulated percussion instruments such as maracas in *Samba de Amigo* (Sonic Team, 1999), bongo drums in *Donkey Konga* (Nintendo, 2004), and a small taiko drum in *Taiko Drum Master* (Namco, 2004). *Guitar Hero* and *Rock Band* use guitar-shaped controllers, while singing-based games using a karaoke-style format, such as *Karaoke Revolution* (Harmonix, 2001) and *SingStar* (London Studio, 2004), require a microphone through which players match pitch in rhythm by singing along with a library of prerecorded popular songs. Nintendo's *Wii Music* (Nintendo, 2008) used a built-in motion controller where players could move their arms in ways that simulated playing a guitar, violin, trumpet, or drums.

Many factors, however, have largely prevented COTS games from being included in the classroom. Many of these games need a dedicated console to play, such as a PlayStation, Xbox, or Nintendo system, which requires a significant financial investment. This does not include the cost of the game itself or any peripherals such as controllers, cameras, and a television or computer monitor. Additionally, only a few students can play these games simultaneously, which would make the ability to have equal class participation difficult given the limited amount of time in a class period. The teacher would also need to review the game for potential inappropriate content, which could be determined from the game's rating.

Nonetheless, teachers and game researchers have not been deterred from exploring the many possibilities that COTS games can bring to the music classroom (Auerbach, 2010; Hein, 2014; Jenson, De Castell, Muehrer, & Droumeva, 2016; Kayali & Pichlmair, 2008; Miller, 2009, 2012; Missingham, 2007; Peppler, Downton,

Lindsay, & Hay, 2011; Roesner, Paisley, & Cassidy, 2016; Tobias & O'Leary, 2016; Wechselberger, 2016). Because COTS games do not contain content that overtly aligns with any state or national standards, educators have had to adapt their curriculum to suit the functionality of individual games. This may be difficult as materials are generally selected to fit the educational objectives rather than modifying the objective for the opportunity to use video games if used simply for the purpose of engaging students.

COTS games are not advertised to ensure that playing them will increase one's instrumental or vocal ability. They rely on the synchronization of rhythmic patterns in combination with pressing the correct sequence of buttons on the controller to loosely simulate instrumental performance. A more appropriate example of software specifically designed to aid instrumental learning would be *Rocksmith* (Ubisoft, 2011), where players use a real guitar to learn and play prerecorded music. However, the expense and difficulty of learning real guitar technique as opposed to the more user-friendly and simplistic design of the *Guitar Hero* controller has resulted in *Rocksmith*'s failure to match the popularity of COTS games (Arsenault, 2008; O'Meara, 2016).

The inability to learn how to play guitar and other instruments through COTS games has not prevented educators from focusing on other aspects of music learning. Instead, playing rhythm-action games can reinforce concepts such as rhythmic interpretation, development of motor skills and hand–eye coordination, and can promote the experience of music-making as part of a collaborative experience (Roesner et al., 2016). Rhythm-action and all music performance games can blur the line between real and recorded by combining the physical gestures of real performances with previously recorded sounds. Although players have no creative input that relates to the actual production of sound, the challenge, visual feedback, and immersion allow musical performance games to engage learners and potentially motivate them to pursue more formal music studies.

Edutainment Games

Unlike games designed solely for entertainment, edutainment, also known as serious games, has a specific predetermined educational objective (Abt, 1970). Edutainment began as an attempt by commercial game designers to enter the educational market by creating video games that reflected COTS games to make them more engaging (Egenfeldt-Nielsen, Smith, & Tosca, 2016). As early as the 1980s, game developers such as Brøderbund, The Learning Company, and Davidson & Associates marketed successful edutainment titles including *Where in the World Is Carmen Sandiego?* (Brøderbund Software, 1985), *Reader Rabbit* (Grimm, 1986), and *Math Blaster!* (Davidson & Associates, 1983).

One of the earliest examples of edutainment that has achieved enduring success is *The Oregon Trail* (Rawitsch, Heinemann, & Dillenberger, 1974), a game created by three teachers to help teach American expansionism during the nineteenth century. (See Figure 2.2.) In this game, the player must make critical decisions from multiple-choice options in order to help guide a family along the Oregon Trail from Missouri. *The Oregon Trail* presented players with a list of options that included purchasing supplies, foraging for food and resources, planning a route, and enduring obstacles such as bad weather, wild animals, and disease. If the player made the wrong series of choices, their characters would perish, and the game would end. However, if the player made the correct choices based on their knowledge of nineteenth-century American geography and history, their characters would reach Oregon successfully.

As such, educators have attempted to use COTS games for educational purposes, including understanding complex systems, solving physics-based equations, and employing strategic decisions (Gee, 2007). Today's edutainment games are normally separated from COTS games as games designed and marketed for purposes other than entertainment. These games span a wide variety of topics, but the term can be used to encompass training, improvement, or marketing (Backlund & Hendrix, 2013).

Edutainment games share some of the design constructs as COTS games, such as a graphical interface, control mechanism, and interaction with an artificial intelligence. The player is rewarded by successfully completing in-game objectives; ideally, this positive reinforcement will then lead to an increased frequency of user achievement (Loftus & Loftus, 1983). It may also increase the player's incentive to achieve more challenging objectives. Many COTS and educational games get more difficult as the player progresses and becomes more proficient at the game. For example, the player may be required to complete certain goals in a reduced amount of time, objectives may become more complicated or involve several stages of completion, or the game may tolerate fewer mistakes before failing the player.

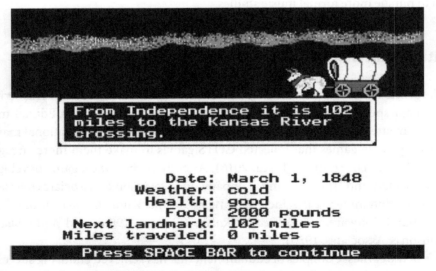

Figure 2.2. *The Oregon Trail* by MECC. Screenshot taken by the author.

Unlike modern COTS games, which can take a significant amount of time to complete, educational games must be designed so that they can be completed within the time span of a lesson or series of lessons, whether within the confines of the classroom or remotely. If played remotely, teachers must have the ability to access the student's progress so that they can be properly evaluated. Educational games and other software services can now be played online or through a dedicated server that automatically transmits this information to the game administrator.

Many edutainment games rely on a repetitive pattern known as skill-and-drill (Dondlinger, 2007). This concept introduces the method of completion to the player and then repeats the same sequence for different problems. Unfortunately, this method of repeated delivery with little to no variation has resulted in diminished interest among students. Critics have labeled edutainment games that have similar structures as "drill-and-kill" (Prensky, 2006; Van Eck, 2006), emphasizing that repeating the same processes no matter how the content is presented will result in the player getting bored and effectively destroying all desire to play.

Many researchers and developers of game-based learning software have identified key areas of how educational games can be designed to promote academic skills without sacrificing player enjoyment. The main concern as to how to accomplish this, however, lies in creating the conditions for enhancing a student's intrinsic motivation to play. A game's challenge plays a major role in determining the player's engagement level; too little challenge and the user will become disinterested, while too much challenge will cause frustration and prompt the user to quit. To this end, game publishers and educational software companies are constantly developing new games that attempt to re-create the enjoyment and engagement provided by popular COTS titles while marketing educational objectives to teachers and administrators.

Classroom Setups

Music teachers, more often than most teachers of other subjects, are usually required to function in a variety of classroom settings. This includes sometimes traveling between classrooms and between different buildings, sharing a classroom, and sometimes not even teaching in a classroom at all. I have experienced all these situations at one point or another during my career, and thus I have had to adapt my teaching methods based on the resources available to me at the time. I have also had the opportunity to teach in my own dedicated classroom where I can organize my materials as I see fit.

Regardless of the environment, the specific equipment needed to implement technology-based learning may also vary. Teachers may be provided with a Smart Board or Smart Panel connected to a single computer, or a computer that is connected to a simple projector. The classroom may have several computers where only a few students can work at a time, or it may have an entire lab of computers for every student in the room. Portable devices, such as laptops, Chromebooks, tablets, or iPads, may be available for a select group of students or the entire class. In many cases, accessing enough portable devices for a whole class requires use of a school-provided cart that must normally be signed out in advance.

Portable devices are now more common since in-person learning after the Covid-19 pandemic was reinstated. Many districts have continued lending students laptops to access online learning platforms such as Google Classroom, Moodle, Canvas, or Blackboard at home. Depending on the teacher or building policy, students may be able to bring their laptops to school for use during class. Many variables need to be examined when planning not just digital game-based learning, but all technology integration in the music classroom. The largest consideration, however, is the type of situation or situations in which the necessary hardware can be accessed on a regular basis (Dammers & LoPresti, 2020).

As discussed in the beginning of this chapter, there are generally four types of classroom technology arrangements: the 1:1 device classroom, the 1: multiple device classroom, the 1 device classroom, and the remote classroom. These situations could change depending on a multitude of factors, including classroom reassignments, availability of devices, devices in need of repair, and other technical difficulties that will be discussed in greater detail later in this chapter. However, teachers will normally find themselves in one of these four circumstances, though the specific type of hardware will vary greatly between school districts.

1:1 Device Environments

The 1:1 device scenario is defined by the opportunity for every student in the class to have individual access to technology during in-person learning, whether it be a desktop computer or a portable device. As mentioned earlier, many districts continued to provide students with laptops after the Covid-19 pandemic subsided and in-person learning returned. The teacher will most likely have their own computer, which will be connected to a Smart Board, Smart Panel, or projector.

If working in a technology lab, each student will be able to work on a dedicated computer that may be linked to a central computer controlled by the teacher. The teacher can then view the content on each student's screen to make sure the student is actively engaged in the lesson or may even control the screen entirely. This is probably the most preferable situation for technology integration, as students can access content on their own but with the regulation of the teacher.

Unfortunately, many school music programs do not have their own dedicated technology lab and would have to schedule use of the school's computer lab based on availability. This could be problematic logistically as many school music teachers see different classes each day and would therefore need to sign out the computer lab every day for all classes to have equal access. Additionally, this would mean that the use of the computer lab would be limited, as other teachers would most likely wish to use the lab for their own classes.

A more likely scenario would be for students to bring in their own district-approved devices into the classroom, whether laptops, Chromebooks, iPads, or tablets, depending on the district. Again, this is also ideal for technology integration, as each student would have access to their own device, though it would prevent the teacher from being able to control them through a central computer. Teachers would need to check student work individually to ensure that they are on-task or would have students post their completed assignments onto an online learning platform.

Since district-approved devices are in most cases connected to the school servers, parental blocking tools will likely be preinstalled to prevent students from accessing inappropriate content. This would be effective for when the device was physically present in the school and was using the school's Wi-Fi account. However, if the student can take the device away from school, those blocking tools may be ineffective if an unprotected Wi-Fi account is used. In any case, it is important to review each website before using it during a lesson for content and accessibility.

1: Multiple Device Environments

If a 1:1 device environment is not possible, many teachers have several computers or portable devices available in the classroom. These can be anything from stand-alone desktop computers to portable devices such as laptops or iPads. Either situation has distinct advantages and disadvantages. First, even though all students cannot simultaneously access technology as a 1:1 device environment provides, a 1: multiple device scenario allows the teacher to retain possession and control of the devices, so they are readily available for all classes. The teacher can set control levels manually so that students stay on task without the risk of viewing inappropriate content. Teachers can also create passwords to prevent students from accessing administrative functions with the support of the district's IT department.

Having portable devices can allow the teacher to manipulate where students will be using them as opposed to a set location like desktop computers. If the teacher wishes to create rotating learning centers, they can decide where the technology station should be in relation to the other groups. However, this will largely depend on the number of devices compared to the number of students in the class. To give all students equal time at each station, they will need to be divided accordingly so that each group has enough devices to accommodate everyone.

For example, if a teacher has 3 iPads and 24 students, there will need to be eight groups to give everyone an equal chance to use the devices. This scenario can present a time management issue, as rotating eight groups between activities in a single class period would be logistically improbable. The teacher could decide to have students progress through the learning stations as part of a multi-lesson unit, but if a student is absent on any given class period, then they will miss one or more stations in the unit. Properly organizing students to use a limited number of devices is paramount for creating an effective experience in which everyone has an equal opportunity to participate.

Another option is to send a group of students to work on the devices independently while the teacher conducts the lesson with the remaining students, and then rotate students based on the number of devices, number of students, and available class time. This allows the teacher to keep track of students more easily, but they will not be able to monitor or assist students using the devices. Additionally, the teacher will not be able to check student work for assessment unless the student can post their completed work onto an online classroom platform or unless the teacher can check students individually at the time of group rotations.

Having a 1: multiple device classroom presents unique opportunities for multitasking and for creating lessons that use numerous ways to present a topic and evaluate for student understanding. It is also more likely to acquire multiple devices for dedicated use in the music classroom than to have a 1:1 device environment that can be employed consistently with all classes. Requesting equipment from the administration or finding external funding for a limited number of devices is much more realistic than attempting to build an entire technology lab. Additionally, should technical difficulties arise, such as loss of the internet, the teacher can simply replace the device station with an alternate activity.

1 Device Environments

The 1 device classroom is a typical setup for many classrooms where the teacher possesses one computer that is connected to a projector device and is displayed to the entire class. In the past, the computer would be linked to a wall projector and would not be able to be manipulated from the board, as is the case with an interactive whiteboard, such as a Smart Board or Smart Panel. The teacher would either need to operate directly from the computer or have a student assistant do it for them Most classrooms are currently equipped with either a Smart Board or a Smart Panel, which allow for a direct interface and can be used from the front of the room.

Even though both Smart Board and Smart Panel possess touchscreens and the ability to draw using digital markers, the main difference between them is that the Smart Panel does not require screen realignment because it is connected directly to the computer. Otherwise, having an interactive whiteboard is extremely beneficial because students can directly observe what the teacher is doing in real time. The potential for student engagement is also increased as they can go directly to the board and work with their peers to solve problems and manipulate digital tools.

A 1 device environment may not be ideal if the goal is to give every student equal access to technology in the time span of a single lesson, but certain strategies may mitigate this disparity. First, students can work in groups or teams and choose a member to go up to work on the board. Digital game-based tools lend themselves well to competitive activities and can foster camaraderie between students as they work to achieve a shared goal.

If the teacher feels that competition may not work effectively for a specific class, then the entire class can act as a single team to complete a task. The competitive element can be introduced as a challenge, such as being able to complete the task in a limited amount of time or using parameters such as communicating without talking. These modifications can help boost teamwork skills and develop leadership qualities through working together for a common purpose.

For games that are more exploratory and focus on creation as the core mechanic, each student can come up to the board individually and add or edit features so that all students can participate. The class size and time allotted will largely determine how long each student can use the board, but teachers can also extend an activity across multiple lessons if they can save the project. A 1 device environment can also be effective as it allows teachers to conduct whole-class lessons and not have to travel to different groups to assess each student individually.

Overall, 1 device environments can help to bring an entire class together, which is very effective for lesson introductions and closings. Since most classrooms have an interactive whiteboard or projector, it may be possible to combine equipment setups in one or multiple lessons, such as using 1 device and multiple devices or beginning with 1 device and then have students work independently on their own devices if a 1:1 environment is available. There are many possibilities to combine and rotate between classroom setups; the choices of which will ultimately depend on the teacher's preferences and knowledge of what strategies are effective in their own unique classrooms.

Remote Environments

Remote classrooms at the public school K–12 level are now mostly used only in times of necessity, such as during the Covid-19 pandemic. However, even when in-person learning was reinstated, hybrid learning was still available in case a student would not be in school for an extended period. Teachers could use online meeting platforms such as Zoom or Google Meet to connect with students while still teaching students who were present in the classroom. While this format presented its own difficulties, such as a lack of participation and potential miscommunications, it still allowed learning to continue in some form as opposed to the alternative of no classroom interactions altogether.

The possibility of returning to a remote learning environment remains, and many school districts are experimenting with different options to blend online with live instruction to accommodate all learning types. Some students and teachers thrive in online classrooms due to less disciplinary distractions, greater freedom of exploration, and greater interaction with technology. In contrast, students have also experienced disadvantages such as procrastination, lack of engagement, and potential technical issues (Major, 2015). Regardless, online learning continues to remain a viable option for not only K–12 schools but is a common format in higher education.

Conducting activities in a remote format usually involves the teacher sharing their screen, sending students materials to an online classroom such as Google Classroom, Canvas, Moodle, or Blackboard, or having students accessing websites on their own. Students can turn in assignments by sending files directly to the teacher via email, posting assignments on the online classroom, sharing their screens so the teacher can visually check for completion, or posting links on the chat board. The most preferable of these alternatives would be for students to turn in assignments on an online classroom tool as the teacher can keep a record of the materials, provide comments directly to the student, and use the grading feature to calculate a student's score. This also retains a student's privacy, as one-on-one communication may not be possible during class.

Students can also be organized into groups or teams using the breakout room feature and be reintegrated into the whole class after a set amount of time. Teachers can also assist individual students using the chat room during times of independent work. The chat room can also be used as a tool for class participation for students who are uncomfortable speaking from behind a computer screen. While some students thrive in communicating online either through voice or text, others may feel more intimidated and will mute their microphones and even turn off their cameras. Even if the teacher requires all cameras to be on during class, some students may feign technical difficulties to prevent others from seeing them.

Since students may not be able to download stand-alone programs due to district blocking software, many activities in an online environment would focus on the use of free websites or downloadable files previously uploaded by the teacher. The student could then complete the work, save a copy of the file, and upload it to the online classroom. Many websites also allow students to save their work and to post a weblink for the teacher to access. The teacher can then grade the work and offer feedback if necessary through text, email, or direct speaking with the student during class in a breakout room. Online classrooms also have an option to invite parents or guardians to view student progress and to maintain communication, which is sometimes easier than sending an email or making a phone call.

Regardless of which of these four learning environments are available, each presents its own set of advantages and disadvantages. Having the choice of which environment to implement is not always possible, and the teacher may need to adapt to whichever situation is mandated at the time. Therefore, it is important to prepare ahead of time by designing lesson plans and assessments that are flexible and can be effective in any situation using materials that are readily available with both technology and nontechnology situations.

Troubleshooting

Any innovation comes with its share of issues that may hinder teachers from incorporating it into the classroom. Although digital games have been available for educational use since the previous century, factors such as curriculum inflexibility, negative stereotypes of gaming, limited budgets, and teacher perceptions of unpreparedness have played a role in the prevention of widespread acceptance (Baek, 2008). Some of these situations, such as financial limitations and lack of administrator support, may be outside of teacher control, but certain strategies can help mitigate these circumstances. This section will discuss some of the common misconceptions of digital gaming in education and how to adapt accordingly.

Technical Issues

All technology-based materials, regardless of whether it is focused on gaming, will have technical difficulties at some point. In a 1:1 device environment, some students will not likely have their equipment due to various reasons, such as they forgot to bring it, the battery was not charged, or the device was under repair. An internet Wi-Fi signal may also be difficult to maintain depending on the location of the room and the school's signal strength. There may also be times when the entire school internet does not function or when materials may not be available.

In these cases, it is important to remember that digital game-based learning, like all technology, is only one tool in a vast array of options for teaching or reinforcing a musical concept. It is not necessary, or even recommended, that technology be used in every lesson, for priority should be placed on giving students a wide variety of musical experiences using diverse materials. Having contingency plans for such an event that can be implemented quickly is vital when plans need to change at a moment's notice. Experienced educators understand that developing alternative plans is part of the rigors of teaching.

In cases of an inability to use digital games in class due to technical difficulties, teachers can provide links for students to access websites at home by posting them on an online classroom program. Teachers can also be proactive by contacting their school's technical support representative and determining the needs of their classroom before beginning lessons using technology. Working with these professionals can reduce the risk of problems by using the right internet browser, having the most updated software, and possessing reliable equipment.

Gaming Controversies

Video games have endured criticisms from political, social, and scientific sources for the past several decades. The most prevalent of these controversies have stated that the prolonged use of video games can cause increased aggression, violent behavior, and addictive tendencies (Anderson & Bushman, 2001; Anderson & Dill, 2000). The 1993 and 1994 congressional hearings on the video game industry explored the potential harm that violent video games could inflict on American youth, though it was ultimately determined that forcing governmental regulation on the sale of video games was a violation of free speech.

However, this investigation gave rise to rating systems such as the ESRB (Entertainment Software Ratings Board), which classifies video games based on age appropriateness. In 2020, the World Health Organization (WHO) labeled "gaming disorder" as a diagnosable disease, defined by "impaired control over gaming, increasing priority given to gaming over other activities to the extent that gaming takes precedence over other interests and daily activities, and continuation or escalation of gaming despite the occurrence of negative consequences" (World Health Organization, 2020).

Teacher adoption of educational games has been hampered by these negative perceptions, though none of these studies has consistently offered conclusive empirical proof of these effects in widespread cases (Böshe & Kattner, 2011). Counterarguments that refute the theory that playing video games causes negative behavioral and psychological effects state that notably few studies involve current violent video games and real children. The primary reasons why children like to play video games include fun, excitement, having something to do when bored, the challenge of figuring things out, and the chance to compete and win, and not because they seek to engage in violent behavior (Kutner & Olson, 2008).

Educational games also do not contain the violence and inappropriate material that COTS games rated as Teen or Mature possess. Communicating this fact to administrators and other stakeholders by providing them with links to appropriate games that plan to be used in lessons will help dispel concerns. It is also important that games are selected because they reinforce the specific musical concept or concepts being taught and help accomplish those objectives.

Teacher Perspectives

Teachers who have limited experience with video games may also feel uncomfortable if they are not familiar with playing themselves. Many of today's COTS have complicated gameplay and control features that would intimidate anyone without prior gaming experience. Games designed for educational purposes should have simple controls that can be understood in a short time. Teachers do not have to be masters at gaming to teach effectively with digital games. In fact, many students are motivated by the prospect of performing better than the teacher and the ability to assist classmates.

As more digital natives enter the teaching field, their familiarity with video games will help to increase its acceptance and widespread use in the classroom (Bensiger, 2012) This does not mean that teachers who do not have experience with video games cannot adapt or use them in their own lessons. Good video games should transcend age, gender, and levels of experience (Archbell, 2009). Teachers' reluctance to implement video games in the past has included finding appropriate educational video games, obtaining technical assistance in installation, and bearing the cost of buying games and consoles. These barriers have largely been dispelled, as free online games designed specifically for education have alleviated the need for dedicated hardware and installation.

Summary

Many theories have been proposed concerning the effectiveness of digital game-based learning and its future in education. Some consider video games as an innovative yet underexplored resource that will only increase in popularity, while others caution against its use because of previous stigma. Over the past several decades, digital games have become more accessible and less reliant on hardware such as gaming consoles, controllers, or other peripherals. While many educators continue to use commercial games and adapt them for learning musical concepts and skills, the availability of free online games designed for classroom use has been a major step toward gaining greater acceptance among both new and veteran teachers.

The next four chapters will highlight specific games representing different aspects of the National Core Arts Standards, including Creating, Performing, Responding, and Connecting. These games are by no means a complete list, and educators are encouraged to find additional games that suit their interests and the needs of their students. Each lesson plan describes ways to implement that game using any of the four classroom setup scenarios, and a tutorial of each game is available on the Oxford University Press website. A full list of the games outlined in this book is in the Appendix.

3
Creating Music With Games

Prelude

There is no doubt that digital technology has revolutionized the process of music creativity; myriad computer-generated tools that can enhance music composition are available both online and as stand-alone programs. In fact, hand-drawn musical compositions have now largely become obsolete in favor of programs such as *Finale*, *Sibelius*, *MuseScore*, *NoteFlight*, and many others. These programs offer a comprehensive set of tools to design fully realized musical scores for performance and publication, which can be used by amateurs and professionals alike (Dammers & LoPresti, 2020).

Because of the meticulous and thorough structure of these programs, users who possess limited knowledge of musical theory along with technology manipulation may find themselves quickly overwhelmed and potentially frustrated. Learning to use these programs to their full potential can require a significant amount of time and commitment. Additionally, the financial cost of these programs is reserved for those who are dedicated to composing, arranging, and producing musical content and is not necessarily meant for casual use. Some of these programs, such as *MuseScore*, offer downloadable free versions, but the number of features provided is reduced in comparison to the paid full version.

I use *Finale* for a variety of compositional and educational projects, but because of the small time I spend with my students in class (40 minutes a day, once a week), in addition to the financial cost of obtaining individual licenses, made it impractical for me to use this program in the classroom environment. I also did not have a 1:1 student/device ratio, since I relied solely on one computer linked to a Smart Board. During the Covid-19 pandemic, however, each of my students was given a school laptop to use during and after remote learning, but even with a new 1:1 device environment, complications still arose. The district network security prevented any direct downloads, so I could not have my students access any programs that were not specifically online.

Therefore, I needed to find free, online-accessible programs that focused on musical composition for multiple levels of learner ability, while at the same time possessing user-friendly mechanics and an interface that promoted enjoyment and immersion. Although this excluded the console-based music games outlined in Chapter 2, these programs used many of the same constructs that are featured in commercial games. Most importantly, student work could be saved and posted not only for assessment purposes, but also for sharing and collaborating with other students (Dillon, 2003).

Because of the subjective nature of music composition, these websites and applications do not feature an embedded evaluation as quantifiable data, so assessing student work would need to be determined by the teacher. The teacher would also be responsible for creating objectives as per the capabilities of the individual program or programs used in each lesson or unit. While this may not necessarily constitute the definition of a game as requiring a competitive element, components of game-based design such as interaction, freedom of exploration, problem solving, and fantasy are all present (Ahmad, 2020; Arrasvuori, 2006).

Depending on whether students have access to an internet-connected device outside of the classroom, the teacher can create homework assignments that can be submitted through online classroom services such as Canvas, Google Classroom, Moodle, and other platforms. Inside the classroom, teachers will be in a variety of situations involving student computer access. As discussed in Chapter 2, this includes 1:1 devices, 1: multiple devices, 1 device, or remote educational environments. Therefore, each entry contains information on how to implement that program in these respective conditions.

Lesson Template Description

Each game outlined in Chapters 3–6 is organized into sections based on the sophistication of their functionality and the musical experience of the user. Games classified as "Beginner" are not necessarily intended solely for earlier grades or developmental levels, though they are designed with a simple user interface and accessibility. Older students may find these games basic and easy to manipulate, but many are still engaged by their interactivity, graphics, and sound creation functions.

"Intermediate" games can be enjoyed by students with a variety of technological and musical experiences, though they require some prior knowledge of how to manipulate the individual system functions of the game. This knowledge can be introduced through a tutorial session with the teacher and can be practiced during class or at home.

Finally, "Advanced" games are more complicated and can be difficult to master without some prior musical knowledge and dedicated practice. However, given the rate at which children learn how to use computer-based functions today, it is not difficult to assume that they most likely achieve proficiency with any of these games within a relatively brief period. Although some students may be able to learn and master these programs on their own, having a teacher to help them understand how to play and troubleshoot potential issues will always result in a more effective learning environment.

Lesson templates are organized by a predetermined set of objectives, though teachers are encouraged to devise alternative goals based on their experience and personal preferences. The objectives are written in accordance with the National Core Arts Standards, but they can be modified and adapted as needed. Suggested lesson activities are presented after a description of each game, followed by accommodation for differentiated instruction. Certain games, such as those described in subsequent chapters, have quantitative evaluations embedded as part of the game's structure. Games that are more exploratory based, such as those presented in this chapter, give sample methods of assessments that can be changed at the teacher's discretion.

The "Level Up!" section offers extensions for further learning opportunities, specifically for those students who excel and are looking for an extra challenge. These extensions can also be used to promote cross-curricular integration and learning beyond the classroom environment. Finally, every program will contain limitations as to any technical or accessibility issues, in addition to modifications that the teacher may have to make to improve the quality and effectiveness of the lesson.

Teachers are also encouraged to use additional supplemental materials, either digital or nondigital, to enhance the lesson based on their own experience and personal preferences. Tutorials and gameplay for each example are also available on the Oxford University Press (OUP) website, and many more are available online. Use whichever games you feel would be most effective for you and your students, and above all, enjoy the experience.

Beginner Games

Game Title: *Rhythm Maker* by Google

Suggested Grade Levels: K–2

Website: https://musiclab.chromeexperiments.com/Rhythm

Objectives: Students will be able to:
- Create and improvise rhythmic patterns using a variety of different timbres and character animations.
- Experiment with rhythmic patterns in different beat structures, including groupings in 3, 4, 5, and 6.

Game Description: *Rhythm Maker* (Figure 3.1) is part of a suite of musical programs by Google Chrome in which users enter different rhythms on a grid as represented by geometric symbols. Some symbols are already present on the grid but can be altered or removed along with placing new rhythms. Clicking the arrows on the side of the screen changes the animation characters along with the number of beats in each grid. There are a total of four grids to choose from, each with its own set of instrumental timbres and character animations.

Video Tutorial: See ▶ Video 3.1 on the OUP Companion Website.

Procedures
- 1:1 Device Environments
  - Students can experiment with rhythmic improvisations on their own or with guidance from the teacher. The teacher can create objectives for students to work within a specific grid or create rhythms that represent quarter, eighth, half, whole, or other combinations of beats. Students can also work collaboratively or independently depending on the teacher's objectives.
- 1: Multiple-Device Environments
  - Students can rotate in groups to develop original rhythmic compositions, then share them with the teacher or the entire class before the next group begins.
- 1 Device Environments
  - The teacher can invite students to the board to create their own compositions and share them with the class. The teacher can also have the class create their own compositions as a group or split the class into four groups and have each group work on a specific grid. The grids do not reset unless the web page is reloaded. Students can also perform along with rhythmic compositions, using body percussion or classroom instruments.
- Remote Environments
  - Students can work independently or as a whole-class environment with teacher guidance using a specific rhythmic design. Students can share their screens and display their rhythms to the class while the other students can evaluate their work. The teacher can provide a rubric for self-evaluation and the evaluation of others' works.

Adaptations
- Students who need extra assistance can be given additional guidance by the teacher. If there are students who demonstrate a high level of aptitude, the teacher can decide to have those students engage in peer-to-peer collaboration, though this may be more difficult in remote environments. Students who show accelerated growth can be given additional objectives as determined by the teacher, such as creating more complex rhythmic patterns, using a specific grid, or creating additional compositions using multiple grids.

Assessments
- Teachers may create evaluation rubrics based on the use of individual rhythmic elements or the completion of tasks, such as creating a rhythm pattern using a specific time signature or beats representing actual notation. This also includes student participation in self-evaluation and evaluation of others' work.

Level Up!
- Students can create rhythmic improvisations representing rhythms of specific songs. For example, students can re-create drumbeats from popular songs or preselected songs chosen by the teacher.

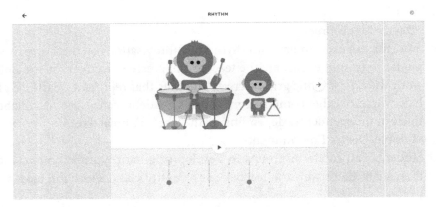

Figure 3.1. *Rhythm Maker* by Google. Screenshot by the author.

Limitations
- *Rhythm Maker* is a basic program that does not allow for a large variety of features. Students may become bored after experimenting a certain amount of time, so this program would not necessarily be suitable for an entire class lesson. Instead, it could be used as an in-class activity as part of a larger lesson.
- There is no save feature, so students cannot post their work online.
- There is no option to change tempo or instrument timbres beyond what is already provided in each grid.

Game Title: *Cyber Pattern Player* **by PBS Kids**

Suggested Grade Levels: K–2

Website: https://pbskids.org/cyberchase/games/cyber-pattern-player

Objectives: Students will be able to:
- Create musical patterns using different melodic and rhythmic combinations on a sequencer grid.
- Create melodies and rhythms using various musical timbres.

Game Description: *Cyber Pattern Player* (Figure 3.2) begins with a brief tutorial showing users how to enter in sounds by clicking boxes in a single grid. When ready, the user can click the next button to access a larger grid of six rows that play different musical timbres. Clicking on each box will play a singular note; clicking on the same box will delete the note. Students can either access a total of four pre-made patterns or create their own using five timbre settings, which are manipulated by clicking the "more sounds" wheel. This information can also be reviewed by clicking the "help" button.

Video Tutorial: See ▶ Video 3.2 on the OUP Companion Website.

Procedures
- 1:1 Device Environments
    - Students can work independently or in groups to create their own melody by either altering the pre-made patterns or starting from a blank grid. Students can walk around the room to listen and evaluate classmates' work using evaluation rubrics.
- 1: Multiple Device Environments
    - Students can rotate in groups to develop original compositions, then share them with the teacher or the entire class before the next group begins.
- 1 Device Environments
    - The teacher can invite students to the board to create their own compositions and share them with the class. The teacher can also have the class create their own compositions as a group or multiple groups. Students can also perform along with rhythmic compositions using body percussion or classroom instruments.
- Remote Environments
    - Students can work independently or as a whole-class environment with or without teacher guidance. Students can share their screens and display their compositions to the class while the other students can evaluate their work. The teacher can provide a rubric for self-evaluation and the evaluation of others' works.

Adaptations
- Students who need extra assistance can be given additional guidance by the teacher. There is also a closed-captioned option for students, which can be accessed at the top of the screen. If there are students who demonstrate a high level of aptitude, the teacher can decide to have those students engage in peer-to-peer collaboration, though this may be more difficult in remote environments.

Assessments
- Teachers may create or use predesigned evaluation rubrics based on the use of individual rhythmic elements or the completion of tasks, such as creating a rhythm pattern using a specific time signature or beats representing actual notation. This also includes student participation in self-evaluation and evaluation of others' work.

Level Up!
- Students can create lyrics to accompany their melodies or play along using body percussion or classroom instruments.

Limitations
- Like *Rhythm Maker, Cyber-Pattern Player* is a basic program that does not allow for a large variety of features. Students may become bored after experimenting a certain amount of time, so this program would not necessarily be suitable for

40 Gamifying the Music Classroom

Figure 3.2. *Cyber Pattern Player* by PBS Kids. Screenshot by the author.

an entire class lesson. Instead, it could be used as an in-class activity as part of a larger lesson.
- There is no save feature, so students cannot post their work online.
- There is no option to change tempo or instrument timbres beyond what is already provided in each grid. Students may also decide to use the pre-made patterns as part of their work, but this does not show any original creativity.

Game Title: *Song Maker* by Google

Suggested Grade Levels: K–4

Website: https://musiclab.chromeexperiments.com/Song-Maker

Objectives: Students will be able to:
- Compose original music using elements such as rhythm, timbre, melody, tempo, and form.
- Evaluate their own and classmates' work using musical terminology and critical thinking.

Game Description: *Song Maker* (Figure 3.3) is an online music sequencer that allows users to create music by placing sounds on a grid. Each grid space represents a different note that can be altered with a different instrumental timbre, including marimba, piano, strings, woodwinds, and synthesized sounds. A percussion track can also be added with electronic, woodblock, drum kit, and conga drum sounds. In the settings menu, users can change the tempo, number of measures, time signature, octave range, and tonal structure. When completed, students can save their work under a general weblink that can be copied and pasted for others to view.

Video Tutorial: See ▶ Video 3.3 on the OUP Companion Website.

Procedures
- 1:1 Device Environments
  - Students can work independently after receiving instructions from the teacher. The teacher can set specific objectives such as free composition or guidelines to use certain parameters such as number of measures, time structure, form, melodic and rhythmic direction, or a combination of instrumental timbres. Students can post their links to an online classroom program such as Google Classroom or email to the teacher directly. The teacher can also have students evaluate their own and others' work using rubrics and music-specific terminology.
- 1: Multiple Device Environments
  - Students can work in self-directed or guided teams to create group projects. They can be individually responsible for elements of composition, or they can work together on the entire project. When finished, students can post their weblinks to an online classroom forum or email to the teacher
- 1 Device Environments
  - The teacher can project the website onto a Smart Board or Smart Panel and have individual students come up to the board and contribute to the overall project. When finished, students can perform a group evaluation or assess the project individually.
- Remote Environments
  - Students can work remotely on the website with or without teacher guidance if needed. Students can then post their work online or send it directly to the teacher. The teacher can then highlight student work and have participants fill out a rubric to evaluate each other. This can either be done as a whole-class activity or as a self-guided gallery "walk."

Adaptations
- Students who need extra assistance can be given additional guidance by the teacher. If there are students who demonstrate a high level of aptitude, the teacher can decide to have those students engage in peer-to-peer collaboration. Students who show accelerated growth can be given additional objectives as determined by the teacher, such as creating more complex rhythmic and melodic patterns and using a specific length of measures, as well as variations of time signatures and scale structure.

Assessments
- Teachers may create evaluation rubrics based on the use of individual musical elements or the completion of tasks. This also includes student participation in self-evaluation and evaluation of others' work.

Level Up!
- If devices have a built-in microphone or if an external microphone is available, students can sing notes into the program.

42   Gamifying the Music Classroom

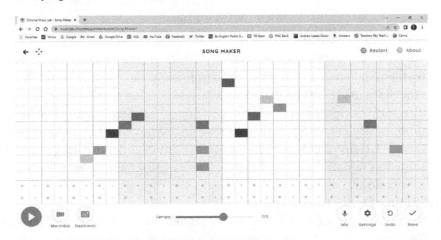

Figure 3.3. *Song Maker* by Google. Screenshot by the author.

- Teachers can use the settings in *Song Maker* to explain scale structures including major, pentatonic, and chromatic. Teachers can also configure the setting menu to teach sharps and flats in addition to differences in octaves.

Limitations
- Only one instrumental sound can be used at a time. If the student changes a sound to a different timbre, prior note entries will also change.
- The microphone feature's effectiveness can vary based on the pitch accuracy of the user.
- The grid entries do not display what pitch has been entered.

Intermediate Games

Game Title: *Online Rhythm Composer* by Inside the Orchestra

Suggested Grade Levels: 3–5

Website: https://insidetheorchestra.org/musical-games/#Rhythmcomposer

Objectives: Students will be able to:
- Create an original rhythm using quarter notes, eighth notes, sixteenth notes, and quarter rests.
- Compare and share their original compositions with other students both online and in person.

Game Description: *Online Rhythm Composer* (Figure 3.4) is part of a suite of website-based games and programs from Inside the Orchestra. Players can enter rhythms by clicking the note symbols provided at the bottom of the screen. They can create short or long rhythms and play them back using the "play" button. The player can also name their song and type their name as the composer. To share a song online, the user can click the button marked "share your song," which will create a weblink that can be copied and pasted.

Video Tutorial: See ▶ Video 3.4 on the OUP Companion Website.

Procedures:
- 1:1 Device Environments
  o Students may work independently or with guidance from a teacher to practice entering in combinations of rhythms. Students may be directed to create rhythms using specific combinations or re-create rhythms of simple songs. Students can also play along to create rhythms using body percussion or classroom instruments. When completed, students may share their rhythms with the teacher or online classroom by copying and pasting the weblink.
- 1: Multiple Device Environments
  o Students can rotate in groups to develop original compositions and then share them with the teacher or the entire class before the next group begins. Students may also be given the option to work together or independently.
- 1 Device Environments
  o The teacher can invite individual students to the board one at a time to create their own rhythms and share them with the class. The teacher can also have the class create their own compositions as a group or multiple groups on the board. The class can then play along with the rhythms using body percussion or classroom instruments, or they can count the beats with the music.
- Remote Environments
  o Students can work independently or as a whole-class environment with or without teacher guidance. Teachers can display and play student work to the class after students post the weblink onto the online classroom platform. Additionally, the teacher can provide a rubric for self-evaluation and the evaluation of others' works during performances. Teachers can also have students count or write the number of beats for each composition during class or for a homework assignment.

Adaptations
- Teachers may need to review rhythm symbols along with their beat assignments with their less advanced students. For advanced students, teachers can have them assist other students or work collaboratively. Additionally, students can play along with their rhythms using classroom resources.

Assessments
- Teachers may create evaluation rubrics based on the completion of tasks, such as creating rhythms using specific beat structures. This also includes using classroom resources to play or count along to student compositions.

Figure 3.4. *Online Rhythm Composer* by Inside the Orchestra. Screenshot by the author.

Level Up!
- Teachers can also use student compositions to reinforce music theory concepts such as staff notation and note values.

Limitations
- The timbre of the song playback is limited to a computerized woodblock sound.
- Users cannot remove rhythms already entered unless they start a new song.
- Users cannot change the tempo as it will automatically be entered as quarter note equals seventy.
- Advanced students may eventually get bored with the limited number of rhythmic combinations available.

Game Title: *Otogarden* by Constantino Oliva

Suggested Grade Levels: 3–6

Website: https://otogarden.com/

Objectives: Students will be able to:
- Improvise musical phrases using the manipulation of a character in a virtually constructed environment.
- Create a variety of musical loops using the sounds of traditional Japanese instruments.

Game Description: In *Otogarden* (Figure 3.5), players take control of a kappa, a creature from Japanese folklore. The kappa wanders in a small garden; navigable in its entirety in a few seconds, the space includes trees, a pond, and patches of flowers and vegetables. Players can freely wander through the garden, as they will encounter no hindrances to their movements. Whenever the kappa contacts one of the garden's landscapes, a musical sound is triggered. The game features musical sounds that represent traditional Japanese instruments, such as the shakuhachi and taiko drum. Players can walk, run, and trigger a loop game mechanic, which will effectively record the players' movements, reproducing them immediately as the button is released. While the length of the loop is set at a duration of 8 seconds, there is no limit to the number of possible concurrent loops (Oliva, 2022).

Video Tutorial: See ▶ Video 3.5 on the OUP Companion Website.

Procedures
- 1:1 Device Environments
  o Students may work independently exploring the sounds of the garden and creating loops using the different instrumental timbres. Teachers may set specific objectives such as the use of timbres or overlap of loops. Students can present their work to the class as a live interactive performance.
- 1: Multiple Device Environments
  o Students can rotate in groups to develop original loops, then present them to the teacher before the next group begins. Students may also be given the option to work together or independently.
- 1 Device Environments
  o The teacher can invite individual students to the board one at a time to create their own loops and share them with the class. The teacher can also have the class create their own compositions as a group or multiple groups on the board as a continuous performance.
- Remote Environments
  o Students can work independently before presenting their work to the class by sharing their screen. Additionally, the teacher can provide a rubric for self-evaluation and the evaluation of others' works during performances.

Adaptations
- The keyboard controls may be initially challenging for less technically experienced students. There is an interface for the use of a standard USB-linked gaming controller, but this has to be purchased separately.

46 Gamifying the Music Classroom

Figure 3.5. *Otogarden* by Constantino Oliva. Screenshot by the author.

Assessments
- Teachers may assign different tasks to be completed, such as using a certain number of instruments or concurrent loops in their compositions. Since the loops disappear after 8 seconds and cannot be saved, teachers need to view students' work as a live performance. The teacher can use this as an opportunity for individual or group class presentations.

Level Up!
- The teacher can use the gameplay presented in *Otogarden* to practice understanding improvisation techniques. Additionally, the teacher can use *Otogarden* as an extension to introduce the world culture music of Japan .

Limitations
- A loop lasts only 8 seconds; after which the loop disappears and is not recorded.
- Loops cannot be saved or shared by a weblink.

Game Title: *Compose Your Own Music* **by Classics for Kids**

Suggested Grade Levels: 3–6

Website: https://www.classicsforkids.com/music-games

Objectives: Students will be able to:
- Use traditional musical notation to compose original melodies.
- Share their own original melodies and self-evaluate or use critical thinking to evaluate the melodies of other students.

Game Description: *Compose Your Own Music* is a simple, web-based program that allows users to enter in combinations of note values using a predetermined set of rhythms. Once selected, users can determine the pitch by choosing a note on the virtual keyboard (flat and sharp notes are not available). After completing a maximum of four measures, students can play back their melodies and share them by copying and pasting a weblink or through email. Each note value is displayed numerically in the note box. Once a note is used, any note that exceeds the number of beats allowed will be unavailable.

Video Tutorial: See ▶ Video 3.6 on the OUP Companion Website.

Procedures
- 1:1 Device Environments
  o Students may work independently or with guidance from a teacher to practice creating melodies that conform to the rhythmic guidelines of 4/4 time. Students may be directed to create music using specific pitch/rhythm combinations, or they may re-create simple songs based on the C Major scale. When completed, students may share their melodies with the teacher or online classroom by copying and pasting the weblink. Since the program only allows for the creation of a maximum of four measures, students may finish quickly and can create multiple compositions.
- 1: Multiple Device Environments
  o Students can rotate in groups to create melodies and then share them with the teacher or the entire class before the next group begins. Students may also be given the option to work together or independently.
- 1 Device Environments
  o The teacher can invite individual students to the board one at a time to create their own melodies and share them with the class. The teacher can also have the class create their own compositions as a group or multiple groups on the board.
- Remote Environments
  o Students can work independently or as a whole-class environment with or without teacher guidance. Teachers can display and play student work to the class after students post the weblink onto the online classroom platform. Additionally, the teacher can provide a rubric for self-evaluation and the evaluation of others' works during performances. Teachers can also have students count or write the number of beats for each composition during class or for a homework assignment.

Adaptations
- There are two versions of the program. The Beginner setting has fewer options for note input (Figure 3.6), whereas the Advanced setting includes dotted note rhythms and other subdivisions. Teachers can decide which version they would like to use with specific students or allow students to choose on their own. It is recommended that students understand 4/4 time along with basic note values before allowing for independent work.

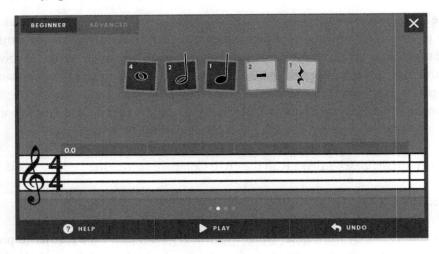

Figure 3.6. *Compose Your Own Music* by Classics for Kids. Screenshot by the author.

Assessments
- Since melodies created on *Compose Your Own Music* can be limited, teachers can evaluate student work based on criteria such as using the structure of the C Major scale to demonstrate knowledge of tonality, or they may require a certain combination of rhythms within each melody. Additionally, teachers can create assessment rubrics so that students can self-evaluate their own work or evaluate the work of other students.

Level Up!
- Teachers can teach the 4/4 conducting technique and have students perform along with each composition. In whole-class environments, teachers can have students accompany melodies with body percussion or instruments. Teachers can also use a traditional notation program such as *Finale*, *Sibelius*, or *Noteflight*, if available, to manually enter in student work and combine them into one large composition.

Limitations
- The only time signature available is 4/4.
- Students cannot choose sharp or flat notes on the virtual keyboard for their melodies.
- Only four measures are available for each melody.
- Students cannot create harmonies or chords.
- Students cannot change the tempo of their compositions.
- When playing melodies, students cannot see the melodies as they are being performed.

Game Title: *Compose with Us Now* by Inside the Orchestra

Suggested Grade Levels: 3–8

Website: https://insidetheorchestra.org/musical-games

Objectives: Students will be able to:
- Create a melody using pitches provided from a virtual keyboard.
- Learn the placement of chromatic notes on the keyboard and on the treble clef staff.
- Compare and share their original compositions with other students both online and in person.

Game Description: *Compose with Us Now* (Figure 3.7) is part of a suite of website-based games and programs from Inside the Orchestra. Users can enter notes by clicking the keys of the virtual piano provided at the bottom of the screen. To remove a note, click the note entered on the screen and then click the "remove note" button that appears on the top right corner. Users can create short or long melodies and play them back using the "play" button. The player can also name their melody and type their name as the composer. To share a melody online, the user can click the button marked "share your song," which will create a weblink that can be copied and pasted.

Video Tutorial: See ▶ Video 3.7 on the OUP Companion Website.

Procedures
- 1:1 Device Environments
  o Students may work independently or with guidance from a teacher to practice associating note names with their places on the staff. Students may be directed to create melodies using specific scale structures and tonalities or to re-create simple melodies. When completed, students may share their melodies with the teacher or online classroom by copying and pasting the weblink.
- 1: Multiple Device Environments
  o Students can rotate in groups to develop original compositions and then share them with the teacher or the entire class before the next group begins.
- 1 Device Environments
  o The teacher can invite individual students to the board one at a time to create their own compositions and share them with the class. The teacher can also have the class create their own compositions as a group or multiple groups on the board.
- Remote Environments
  o Students can work independently or as a whole-class environment with or without teacher guidance. Teachers can display and play student work to the class after students post the weblink onto the online classroom platform. Additionally, the teacher can provide a rubric for self-evaluation and the evaluation of others' works during performances.

50   Gamifying the Music Classroom

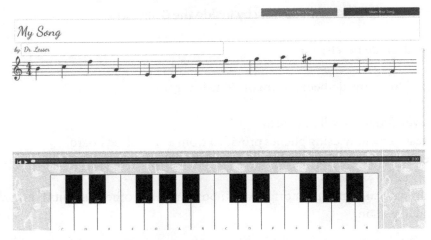

Figure 3.7. *Compose with Us Now* by Inside the Orchestra. Screenshot by the author.

Adaptations
- Note letters are provided on the virtual keyboard for students who need reminders, though the black keys only display one of the two enharmonic names. Additionally, note names are not displayed on the staff when they are selected as part of the melody. Teachers may need to provide students with a resource sheet containing a list of note names as they appear on the staff. Advanced students can create melodies using various keys and tonal structures.

Assessments
- Teachers may create or use predesigned evaluation rubrics based on the completion of tasks, such as creating a melody using specific guidelines. This also includes student participation in self-evaluation and evaluation of classmates' work.

Level Up!
- The teacher can conduct pitch matching exercises or vocalizations using different student compositions. Teachers can also use student compositions to reinforce music theory concepts, such as staff notation and diatonic/chromatic tonality.

Limitations
- There is not a variety of musical timbres that can be used; only the piano sound is available.
- The website does not provide an option for learning or working with bass clef notes.
- Enharmonic notes are not displayed on the black keys of the virtual keyboard.
- Only monophonic melodic content, not harmonies, is available.

Game Title: *Incredibox* by So Far So Good

Suggested Grade Levels: 3–8

Website: https://www.incredibox.com/; it can be downloaded as an app.

Objectives: Students will be able to:
- Create their own musical loops using combinations of prerecorded vocalizations representing various rhythmic and melodic phrases.
- Compare and share their original compositions with other students both online and in person.

Game Description: *Incredibox* is a drag-and-drop program that can operate both online and from a portable iOS device. Users have a choice of 20 different beatboxing sounds to place into seven available characters. These sounds range from rhythmic figures to short melodic phrases, sound effects, or vocalizations. When selected, the character will begin a repeated loop, while the user can add, mute, or remove sounds in different combinations. The loop will continue indefinitely, but it can be paused or stopped at any time. There are several versions representing different musical styles, such as the R&B-inspired "Little Miss," or "Brazil," which has a distinctly Latin sound. Each version has the same gameplay features and can switch at any time. Players can also record up to three minutes of their mixes and share via email or a weblink. If using the app, saved mixes can download as an mp3 file (not available with the website version).

Video Tutorial: See ▶ Video 3.8 on the OUP Companion Website.

Procedures
- 1:1 Device Environments
   o Students can choose the version of *Incredibox* to work with, or the teacher can assign one based on stylistic preference. The teacher can give specific guidelines as to which sound categories to use, or the teacher can have students experiment with different combinations on their own. Students can also work collaboratively to create their own mix and then save it as a weblink after recording. The teacher can next have students post the weblink as part of an email or on an online classroom platform. Students can then self-evaluate or view each other's work and critique using a rubric designed by the teacher.
- 1: Multiple Device Environments
   o Teachers who use laptops or desktop computers can only use the first four versions: "Alpha," "Little Miss," "Sunrise," and "The Love." If the teacher possesses iPads, tablets, or other iOS devices, they will need to download the app, which costs $4.99 per license. This will allow all eight versions to become available. Students can rotate in groups or individually to use *Incredibox* for an amount of time to create and post their work.

- 1 Device Environments
  - ○ The teacher can invite each student to the board to select their own sound and use them in combination as part of a whole-class performance. Students can also perform along with rhythmic compositions using body percussion or beatboxing. When finished, the teacher can hold a performance by having students select their choices while in the process of recording. Students can then evaluate their own mix and mixes of other classes.
- Remote Environments
  - ○ Students can work independently with or without teacher guidance. Students can post their links onto an online classroom program and play their compositions to the class, while the other students can evaluate their work. The teacher can provide a rubric for self-evaluation and the evaluation of others' works. This can be done as part of an in-class lesson or as a homework assignment.

Adaptations
- Tutorials are available as part of the website introduction, which can be accessed at any time by clicking the "i" icon at the top right-hand corner of the webpage. Students who demonstrate aptitude and excel at using the program can create multiple mixes if time allows.

Assessments
- The teacher can incorporate assignments such as using a certain amount of rhythmic or melodic phrases or creating a mix that uses a specific number of sound combinations. Students can also evaluate their own work or their classmates by completing a predesigned rubric.

Level Up!
- Selecting a specific combination of five sounds will access one of three bonus songs, which are shortcut scenes that students can view. The bonus song wheels are located above the main gameplay area (Figure 3.8). Students can incorporate one or all of the bonus songs into their recordings as they are unlocked. Playing with *Incredibox* can also segue into topics such as beatboxing, a cappella singing, or multiple musical genres, including hip-hop, R&B, Latin, and pop.

Limitations
- While the website version is free, only the first four of the eight themes are available. Downloading the app allows all eight themes to be accessed but at a cost of $4.99 per license.
- Upon beginning the game, the cartoon characters do not wear shirts until the player chooses a sound. This may be considered inappropriate for younger students.
- Mixes that are saved cannot be downloaded as an mp3 file using the website version.

Creating Music With Games 53

Figure 3.8. *Incredibox* by So Far So Good. Screenshot by the author.

- The maximum amount of time that a song can be recorded for is three minutes. This may not be sufficient when using *Incredibox* as part of a whole-class lesson with one device.

Advanced Games

Game Title: *Compose It* by New Bedford Symphony Orchestra

Suggested Grade Levels: 4–8

Website: https://nbsymphony.org/compose-it/

Objectives: Students will be able to:
- Create original melodies or re-create existing melodies using a variety of rhythmic and pitch combinations.
- Self-evaluate and critique the work of others using critical thinking and musical terminology.

Game Description: *Compose It* (Figure 3.9) is a free web-based program that allows users to create their own music using a drag-and-drop format into a sequencer grid. Users can choose a variety of rhythms to create melodies using traditional notation in either 3/4 or 4/4 time and have it played back by clicking the "play" button. When finished, students can either clear their melodies or save a copy as a PNG file and print or share with others.

Video Tutorial: See ▶ Video 3.9 on the OUP Companion Website.

Procedures
- 1:1 Device Environments
    - Students may work independently or with guidance from a teacher to practice creating melodies that conform to the rhythmic guidelines of 4/4 or 3/4 time. Students may be directed to create music using specific pitch/rhythm combinations, or they may re-create simple songs based on diatonic tonal structures. When completed, students may share an image of their melodies to the teacher or online classroom by downloading and sending the file through email. Since the program only allows for the creation of a maximum of three measures, students may finish quickly and can create multiple compositions in both time signatures.
- 1: Multiple Device Environments
    - Students can rotate in groups to create melodies and then download them and send an email to the teacher or the entire class before the next group begins. Students may also be given the option to work together or independently.
- 1 Device Environments
    - The teacher can invite individual students to the board one at a time to create their own melodies and share them with the class. The teacher can also have the class create their own compositions as a group or multiple groups on the board.
- Remote Environments
    - Students can work independently or as a whole class environment with or without teacher guidance. Students can display and play student work to the class using screen-share. Additionally, the teacher can provide a rubric for self-evaluation and the evaluation of others' works during performances.

Adaptations
- The program offers an in-game menu that can be accessed through the "help" button at the bottom left corner of the screen. A video tutorial can also be viewed by scrolling below the program and clicking on the video titled "Introducing Compose-it." Students can also change between using rhythmic notation or colored grid lines by clicking the "notation" button.

Assessments
- Many lesson activities are available on the *Compose It* website, or teachers can design their own lesson objectives by having students create melodies according to certain criteria. This may include using a certain number of rhythmic values or a specific tonal structure. Teachers may also have students share screenshots of their melodies and evaluate them using predesigned rubrics.

Creating Music With Games 55

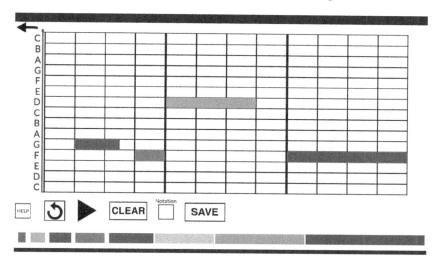

Figure 3.9. *Compose It* by New Bedford Symphony Orchestra. Screenshot by the author.

Level Up!
- The *Compose It* website offers weekly supplemental lesson videos that can be accessed by scrolling down the webpage. These videos include analyzing the melodies and content of significant musical works, music theory exercises, and connections to STEM-related subjects.

Limitations
- No sharp or flat pitches are available, and notes cannot be layered in harmonic structures.
- The only timbre available for playback is a computerized piano sound.
- Students can only compose up to three measures.
- Students cannot save or share audio recordings of their work.

Game Title: *Mario Paint Composer* **by unfun Games**

Suggested Grade Levels: 4–8

Website: https://minghai.github.io/MarioSequencer (Online); https://www.mariomayhem.com/downloads/mario_paint_composer_download (Download)

Objectives: Students will be able to:
- Create original music or arrangements of preexisting songs using a combination or traditional and nontraditional notation in 4/4 or 3/4 time.
- Self-evaluate and critique the work of others using critical thinking and musical terminology.

Game Description: In 1992, Nintendo released *Mario Paint* (Figure 3.10) on the Super Nintendo console, which was a nontraditional exploratory game featuring the character of Mario. Players could engage in multiple activities, including a drawing board, coloring book, animation designer, and a music composition sequencer. The composition feature allowed users to create their own music using icons representing Nintendo icons from the *Super Mario Bros.* game series and place them on a traditional music staff. Users could play back their work and save them onto the console for future listening. Although there have been no updates or remakes of *Mario Paint* from Nintendo, several re-creations of the *Mario Paint* composer feature have been subsequently released online. The *Mario Sequencer*, developed by GitHub, does not require any downloads and is a faithful emulator of the original program. A free downloadable version, created by unfun Games in 2008, has the same construct as the online version, but it allows users to save and load their work if there is enough memory space on the computer. *Mario Paint Composer* can work on Windows or Mac-based devices, including computers, laptops, MacBooks, or Chromebooks. Over the last several years, an online community based on creating music using *Mario Paint Composer* has emerged on YouTube and sites such as the *Mario Paint Composer* Hangout at https://mariopaintcomposer.proboards.com/.

Video Tutorial: See ▶ Video 3.10 on the OUP Companion Website.

Procedures
- 1:1 Device Environments
  - Students may work independently or with guidance from a teacher to practice creating melodies in either 4/4 or 3/4 time. Students may be directed to create music using specific pitch/rhythm combinations or re-create simple songs using examples from YouTube or the *Mario Paint Composer* Hangout. When completed, teachers may have students complete a gallery walkthrough by rotating around the room and listening to each other's compositions. Teachers may also provide students with an evaluation rubric to critique classmates' work.
- 1: Multiple Device Environments
  - Students can rotate in groups to create songs, then create a video recording and post it to an online classroom platform before the next group begins. Students may also be given the option to work together and submit a group project.
- 1 Device Environments
  - The teacher can invite individual students to the board one at a time to contribute to a larger overall class composition. The teacher can also have the class create their own compositions as a group or multiple groups on the board using rotating groups.

- Remote Environments
  o Students can work independently or as a whole-class environment with or without teacher guidance. Students can display and play student work to the class using screen-share. Additionally, the teacher can provide a rubric for self-evaluation and the evaluation of others' works during performances. Students can also create a video recording of their work and post it to an online classroom forum.

Adaptations
- There are many online resources to explore different compositional techniques with *Mario Paint Composer*. YouTube contains an abundance of songs published by experienced users in which students can gain inspiration. Instructional tutorial videos are also available for students who are first learning the program or for advanced users who wish to learn more complicated composition techniques.

Assessments:
- Teachers can design their own lesson objectives by having students create compositions according to certain criteria or re-create preexisting songs. Teachers may also have students perform their work during class and evaluate them using predesigned rubrics.

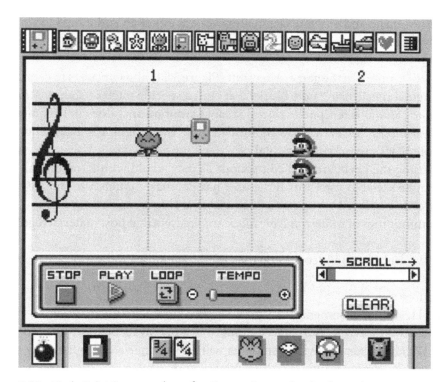

Figure 3.10. *Mario Paint Composer* by unfun Games. Screenshot by the author.

58 Gamifying the Music Classroom

Level Up!
- Students can look up *Mario Paint Composer* songs on YouTube and evaluate selections based on predetermined musical criteria as directed by the teacher. Students can also visit the *Mario Paint Composer* Hangout and read posts or listen to compositions.
- The teacher can use *Mario Paint Composer* as a segue to introduce topics such as video game music, chiptune music, or other forms of electronic music.

Limitations
- Students can save songs only when they are using the downloadable version. However, students can only play songs from the program and cannot send or share them unless they record them as a video file.

Game Title: *Minecraft Open Note Block Studio* **by Open NBS**

Suggested Grade Levels: 5–8

Website: https://opennbs.org/ (free Windows download)

Objectives: Students will be able to:
- Create, edit, and save original music using *Minecraft* note blocks representing different pitches and percussive sounds.
- Self-evaluate and evaluate classmates' work as either an audio mp3 file or visually with *Minecraft*.

Game Description: In the game, *Minecraft* (Figure 3.11) allows players to create their own original music using note blocks that emit a specific pitch or sound. *Minecraft Note Block Studio* is a separate downloadable program that does not require purchasing *Minecraft* or even knowing how to play. The program is a sequencer that uses note blocks representing a total of sixteen musical sounds. Users can enter in blocks using the keyboard and edit sounds as they would with a traditional DAW. Files can be saved as mp3's, or if the user has purchased *Minecraft*, the file can be converted to be played in the game. Many tutorial videos can be found online, along with communities of *Minecraft Note Block Studio* users that post material regularly.

Video Tutorial: See ▶ Video 3.11 on the OUP Companion Website.

Procedures
- 1:1 Device Environments
  o Since *Minecraft Note Block Studio* is only available for download on Windows-based devices, students will need either a computer or a laptop with a Windows interface. This may require using a school computer lab or

borrowing a laptop cart if one is available. Students may work independently or with guidance from a teacher to practice creating and editing music. Students may be directed to work independently or collaboratively in either free composition or completion of specific tasks. When completed, teachers may have students perform a gallery walkthrough by rotating around the room and listening to each other's compositions, or teachers may have students send their completed files by posting on an online classroom forum. Teachers may also provide students with an evaluation rubric to self-evaluate or critique classmates' work.

- 1: Multiple Device Environments
  o Students can rotate in groups to create songs using computers or laptops, and then save the completed file and post it to an online classroom platform before the next group begins. Students may also be given the option to work together and submit a group project. After all students have been given an opportunity to work on the program, which may take multiple lessons to complete based on the number of students in the class, the teacher can play each individual work and have students self-evaluate and critique others' compositions.
- 1 Device Environments
  o The teacher can invite individual students to the board one at a time to contribute to a larger overall class composition. The teacher can also have the class create their own compositions as a group or multiple groups on the board using rotating groups. If students have access to *Minecraft Note Block Studio* on a home device, teachers can play student work and use evaluation rubrics for critique.
- Remote Environments
  o Students will need to download *Minecraft Note Block Studio* onto their devices or home computers to run the program. This may or may not be available, depending on whether students have Windows-based computers or laptops at home. If so, teachers can have students work independently after receiving instructions on how to use the program. Students can then send completed work to the teacher and the teacher can play them using *Minecraft Note Block Studio* for the class. Students can also save their files as an mp3 and email it to the teacher or post it in an online classroom format. Teachers can then have students either self-evaluate their work or evaluate their classmates' work by filling out a predesigned rubric.

Adaptations

- *Minecraft Note Block Studio* is an advanced DAW that requires tutorials before students will be able to access its full capabilities. Although many online tutorials can be viewed on YouTube, it may be more effective for the teacher to spend as much time as needed to ensure understanding. It may take several lessons for students to fully explore the program, so it is important to consider the availability of laptops and computers for multiple uses.

Gamifying the Music Classroom

Assessments
- Teachers can design their own lesson objectives by having students create compositions according to certain criteria or re-create preexisting songs. Teachers may also have students share their work during class and evaluate them using predesigned rubrics. Students can also post their work as mp3 files to an online classroom forum and share them with classmates.

Level Up!
- *Minecraft* is available through either console-based systems, mobile iOS systems, or online for $29.99. Should the teacher wish to purchase *Minecraft*, songs created in *Minecraft Note Block Studio* can be converted and imported into the game. Students can then see their compositions presented as part of the game. This is a unique feature and is not available with any other DAW. It can create new pathways of understanding through the connection of music and digital games.

Limitations
- *Minecraft Note Block Studio* is available for download only on Windows-based computers.
- Songs created in *Minecraft Note Block Studio* can only be played in *Minecraft* if the user has purchased the game.
- The sound quality of *Minecraft Note Block Studio* is basic Musical Instrument Digital Interface (MIDI) and is not as sophisticated as some advanced DAWs like *Garageband* or *Mixcraft*.

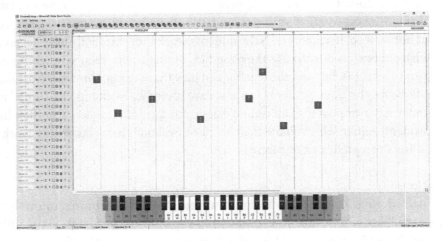

Figure 3.11. *Minecraft Open Note Block Studio* by Open NBS. Screenshot by the author.

Summary

In this chapter, we discussed games that allow players to create, edit, and share their own original music using combinations of traditional and nontraditional notation. While this may not conform to the definition of games as commonly described—as competitive settings that result in a winner or loser—the rise of games as vehicles for exploration without the possibility of failure has grown in popularity as per the examples presented in Chapter 2. Chapter 4 will present games that focus on music performance using various means of player interface. Many of these games provide an embedded assessment and quantitative scoring system that players and teachers can use to evaluate progress in real time.

4
Performing Music With Games

Prelude

When Harmonix released *Guitar Hero* in November 2005, players immediately immersed themselves in the experience of being able to play music without the time and practice necessary to master a real instrument. The line between real and simulated musical performance suddenly became more ambiguous, leading to critics both lauding and condemning this new genre (Miller, 2009). Nearly 20 years later, the rhythm action category of video games has continued to thrive, with dozens of titles created for video game consoles, computers, and handheld devices.

The graphics, interface, and content of rhythm action games have greatly varied over the past two decades, but rhythm action games in general share several qualities that have defined the genre and connected their game mechanics. Pichlmair and Kayali (2007) identified several aspects of rhythm action games that are common throughout the genre. First, rhythm action games usually have an active musical score, displayed in various forms of nontraditional notation, which changes in real time according to the player's actions in combination with the background music. Players also receive a quantitative score based on their ability to correctly perform these actions as defined by the game's structure.

Rhythm action games also provide quantization, or the alignment of a sound or command to fit within the visual interface. This effect can vary greatly between games, such as arrows in *Dance Dance Revolution* or buttons on a simulated guitar in *Guitar Hero* (Arsenault, 2008; Auerbach, 2010; Smith, 2004). This visual stimulation, along with the aural prompts, can create a state of synesthesia, or the condition of merging two senses that causes involuntary reactions in both, such as "seeing" sound or "hearing" shapes. This condition is also influenced by the physical act of performance, which is required to advance through the game.

Other parameters that can vary between games include overall speed of the game, type of game objects, number of game objects, movement of objects, timing and frequency of objects, removal of objects, and operative rules, goals, and scoring principles (Arrasvuori & Holm, 2010). The music is always accompanied by graphics that are designed to visually represent sound. Using these features, rhythm action games blend active and passive musical content by combining the physical gestures of real performances with previously recorded sounds (Miller, 2009).

In many music games, playing without an objective or penalties, known as free form, is also available for the sheer act of creative performance. The beginner games featured in this chapter fit this category, as players are not scored based on the number of notes or rhythms they input correctly. This approach eliminates the fear of failure and focuses more on the act of playing various musical sounds in creative ways. For older students, challenge and competition can serve as a motivating factor, whether it is against the game's system or an opponent (Gower & McDowell, 2012; Missingham, 2007). The games highlighted in the Intermediate and Advanced Games sections offer progressive levels of difficulty and rewards for completing objectives, such as unlocking extra musical content and sharing high scores online.

Beginner Games

Game Title: *Carmen's World Orchestra* by PBS Kids

Suggested Grade Levels: PreK–2

Website: https://pbskids.org/luna/games/carmens-world-orchestra

Objectives: Students will be able to:
- Identify and play samples of instruments representing India, Egypt, and Mexico.
- Improvise and perform combinations of melodic content using prerecorded instrumental sounds.

Game Description: *Carmen's World Orchestra* (Figure 4.1) is based on the PBS Kids series "Let's Go Luna!" and features characters such as Luna, Andy, Carmen, and Leo. Luna performs an animated dance based on the instruments that the player chooses, which include both the instruments played by the other characters and a bank of extra instruments at the bottom of the screen. Players can choose a set of instruments representing India, Egypt, and Mexico while earning bonus Luna dancing animations. After a certain amount of time, players can take a picture or print their current screen.

Video Tutorial: See ▶ Video 4.1 on the OUP Companion Website.

Procedures
- 1:1 Device Environments
  o Students may explore the program on their own after receiving a brief tutorial from the teacher. Students can be directed as to which instruments they should use or be allowed to freely explore instruments at their own pace. When completed, students can share their improvisations with the teacher or the entire class as part of a group performance.

- 1: Multiple Device Environments
    - Students can work together to create joint performances that can be performed on a Smart Board, laptop, or iPad/tablet. Students can create their own performances and share with the class. Students can also use predesigned rubrics to evaluate their own performances and those of their classmates.
- 2 Device Environments
    - Teachers can invite students to the device individually or as a group to create a performance and share with the class. Students can use predesigned rubrics to evaluate their own performances and those of their classmates.
- Remote Environments
- Students can work independently or as a whole-class environment with or without teacher guidance. Students can play their own work to the class or screen-record their performance and send it to the teacher. Additionally, the teacher can provide a rubric for self-evaluation and the evaluation of others' works during performances.

Adaptations
- Teachers may wish to focus on a particular instrument, country, or instrumental group (percussions, strings, etc.) when introducing the program.
- Teachers can also have students match the instrumental sound to a pattern created by the teacher or other students.

Assessments
- Teachers can quiz students on matching instrumental sounds with their country of origin, their name, or image. Students can also perform their improvisations individually or in groups for the whole class.

Level Up!
- Teachers can intersperse, using the program with YouTube clips of performances from selected instruments or examples of songs from various cultures.
- Teachers can have students play examples of familiar songs using ethnic instruments if available.

Limitations
- Players cannot skip or stop the in-game narration, which can be tedious in multiple sessions or when trying to sample instruments.
- Players have a limited time to perform and improvise before the end of the game. However, students can reset the game and begin again as many times as needed.
- Students can only see an image of their work and cannot listen to an mp3 file.

Performing Music With Games   65

Figure 4.1. *Carmen's World Orchestra* by PBS Kids. Screenshot by the author.

Game Title: *Peg + Cat Music Maker* **by PBS Kids**

Suggested Grade Levels: PreK–2

Website: https://pbskids.org/peg/games/music-maker

Objectives: Students will be able to:
- Perform an original melodic creation using different notes, tempos, and instrumental accompaniments.
- Create a melodic ostinato using various pitches representing one or more different available themes.

Game Description: *Peg + Cat Music Maker* (Figure 4.2) is based on the PBS Kids show "Peg + Cat." Players can choose among three different settings: the bamboo grove, the junkyard, and the magical forest. Each location features melodic loops of eight notes that the player can change by clicking and dragging an animated pillar up or down. As Cat walks across the screen, each note will play in sequence in a repeated pattern. The player can change the tempo of the melody from slow to medium or fast, and can also have Peg play along by clicking the instrument at the bottom of the screen. Players can continue to change pitch while the melody is playing, creating a variety of performance opportunities.

Video Tutorial: See ▶ Video 4.2 on the OUP Companion Website.

Procedures
- 1:1 Device Environments
  - Teachers can have students work independently after completing a brief tutorial explaining how to use the program. The teacher can choose which one of the three themes the students will be working on, or they can let the students choose their own theme or themes as time allows. Students can create their own melodies with one or more themes as directed by the teacher, who may wish to set specific parameters on the melodies or may let the students create their melodies freely. Teachers may also wish to conduct a whole-class lesson where students can re-create melodies predetermined by the teacher. Students can also give performances of their melodies for the whole class or in smaller groups.
- 1: Multiple Device Environments
  - Teachers can have students work in smaller groups as collaborative performances and rotate between different groups if time allows. Each group can give a performance of their work at the conclusion of the activity, which students can evaluate using predesigned rubrics.
- 1 Device Environments
  - Teachers can invite individual students to the board to create a collaborative performance by having them change one note per turn while the music is playing. Depending on the size of the class and the time allotted, students may have multiple turns.
- Remote Environments
  - Students can work independently or as a whole-class environment with or without teacher guidance. Students can play their own work to the class or screen-record their performance and send it to the teacher. Additionally, the teacher can provide a rubric for self-evaluation and the evaluation of others' works during performances.

Adaptations:
- Teachers may wish to provide headphones for students with sensory needs, particularly if they are working with multiple devices.
- Teachers can have more advanced students work in pairs with students who require additional support.

Assessments
- Teachers can direct students to create melodies according to specific parameters, such as using a variety of pitches or ostinatos.
- Teachers can use rubrics and critical thinking for students to self-evaluate their own performances and those of their classmates.

Figure 4.2. *Peg + Cat Music Maker* by PBS Kids. Screenshot by the author.

Level Up!
- Teachers can use the instruments and themes featured in the game, such as the shamisen, to explore world cultures, myths, and legends.
- Teachers can build or have students bring in instruments from household materials to create a "junk band" orchestra and play along to the junkyard theme.
- Teachers can use the numbers designating each piece as an avenue to introduce basic math concepts.

Limitations
- Players cannot save or download their work.
- Students cannot change the number of notes in the ostinato or create different rhythms.

Game Title: *Slap Track* by HoneyDooDat Productions

Suggested Grade Levels: K–2

Website: https://slaptrack.honeydoodat.com/tabs/slaptrack

Objectives: Students will be able to:
- Perform in different rhythmic combinations using various motions and body percussion.
- Perform body motions in sequence with different time signatures and tempos.

Game Description: *Slap Track* (Figure 4.3) is a music performance game like traditional rhythm action games in commercial video games. Players clap, tap, and perform other physical motions in time with the music. The game can be customized for different tempos and time signatures, and the frequency of specific gestures or body motions can be customized. The game begins in 4/4 time but can be changed to any simple or complex time signature. The game will continue until the player manually stops the sequence.

Video Tutorial: See ▶ Video 4.3 on the OUP Companion Website.

Procedures
- 1:1 Device Environments
  o Teachers will need to monitor individual student progress because students cannot save or share their work. This method may therefore be best used for student practice and to enhance their ability to customize their experiences for greater challenge. Students can also work together in groups to practice based on ability level.
- 1 Multiple Device Environments
  o Students can work individually or in groups as part of rotating stations, but teachers will once again need to evaluate students by direct observation. It may be difficult depending on the number of students in the class and time available. Students can still customize their gameplay, or the teacher can set clear parameters as to the time signature and tempo.
- 1 Device Environments
  o Teachers can have the class perform the game individually or in groups. Teachers can also separate students into teams and have them compete against each other. They will need to score students manually as the game does not have an embedded scoring system and will not end until the teacher stops the game. Teachers can change settings at any time and have students practice different time signatures at various tempos.
- Remote Environments
  o Students will need to be visible on the screen and unmuted to hear the different body percussion patterns. They can be given the opportunity to practice on their own and customize settings to their own preferences. Teachers may wish to form breakout groups to evaluate students more easily, for attempting to view every student on the screen and evaluate them individually may be challenging.

Adaptations
- Students who have difficulty processing physical movements can use any single or multiple motions depending on their ability. Teachers can customize the movements so that certain motions appear more frequently or varied for more advanced students. Teachers can also change to "dark mode" depending on the classroom lighting. In addition, tempos can be customized for students who need additional practice.

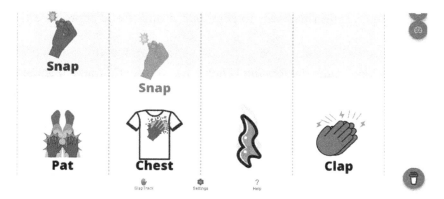

Figure 4.3. *Slap Track* by HoneyDooDat Productions. Screenshot by the author.

Assessments
- Teachers will need to evaluate students individually as they perform to each level. This evaluation can be done individually or in groups. The teacher will need to set up a scoring system to quantify student progress and determine how many rounds to play based on the time available.

Level Up!
- Students can invent new body percussion rhythms, or teachers can have students play with instruments or vocal sounds.
- Students can create their own settings and play the game with their classmates.
- Teachers can use *Slap Track* to introduce the time signature as an important aspect of music notation.

Limitations
- There is no scoring system or direct interface with the game.
- The game does not stop until the teacher or player ends the game manually.

Intermediate Games

Game Title: *Match the Rhythm* by Classics for Kids

Suggested Grade Levels: 3–5

Website: https://www.classicsforkids.com/music-games

Objectives: Students will be able to:
- Perform various combinations of rhythms using a mouse, computer keyboard, and touchscreen by following circles as they scroll across the staff.

- Use aural perception to listen to rhythmic prompts and reproduce them in real time.

Game Description: *Match the Rhythm* (Figure 4.4) is a rhythm-action game played by clicking or using a touchscreen to correctly input rhythms displayed as circles as they scroll across the screen. The game provides a listening example using a drum set playing various rhythms before the player is required to reproduce the rhythms as they cross a vertical bar line. There are customizable options, such as a beginner and advanced mode, in addition to an option for a visual aid.

Video Tutorial: See ▶ Video 4.4 on the OUP Companion Website.

Procedures
- 1:1 Device Environments
  - Students can begin completing levels as a class or individually after receiving a tutorial from the teacher. Teachers can intersperse levels with discussion and practice of simple to complex rhythmic patterns using the game and/or body percussion or instruments. Teachers can also alternate between using the game and exercises with traditional music notation. Since the game is short, the teacher should have other activities prepared for the remainder of the lesson.
- 1: Multiple Device Environments
  - Students may rotate in groups completing levels while the teacher checks for completion. Students may need to work individually as only one person can click or tap the screen at a time.
- 1 Device Environments
  - The teacher can project the game onto a computer screen, Smart Board, or Smart Panel. If a touchscreen is available, students may come up to the board and play one at a time. If a touchscreen is not available, students can use the computer mouse to play. Teachers can alternatively play the game, with the entire class using body percussion or instruments.
- Remote Environments
  - Students can complete levels independently and share their screens with the teacher to show completion. Another option is for the teacher to project the game onto the screen and have students clap or use body percussion to play along with the game and assess students visually. This can be done with students playing individually, in groups, or as a whole class.

Adaptations
- *Match the Rhythm* has both a beginner and advanced difficulty level. The beginner levels use primarily quarter note and eighth note rhythms while the advanced levels use sixteenth notes and combinations of various rhythms.
- The player can use a visual aid that shows rhythms displayed as circles scroll across the screen. When the visual aid is turned off, only the sound of the rhythm

Figure 4.4. *Match the Rhythm* by Classics for Kids. Screenshot by the author.

will be present, in which players will have to reproduce the rhythm using aural perception.
- Students with physical disabilities can say the rhythm or use another form of communication while the teacher or another student plays the game with them.

Assessments
- Levels are completed by correctly reproducing each rhythm in time with the beat. Teachers can view students as they complete levels in either mode. Teachers can also evaluate students by completing a set of levels using either visual or nonvisual aids.

Level Up!
- Teachers can have students play along together to each level by using body percussion or instruments.
- Teachers can use *Match the Rhythm* as a segue to discuss and practice traditional rhythmic notation.

Limitations
- The game displays circles in place of traditional music notes and rhythms.

Game Title: *Rhythm Cat* and *Rhythm Cat 2* by Melody Cats

Suggested Grade Levels: 3–5

Website: https://melodycats.com/rhythm-cat/ (free download for *Rhythm Cat Lite*, $4.99 for *Rhythm Cat* full version)

Objectives: Students will be able to:
- Identify different examples of notes representing traditional music notation in various rhythmic patterns.
- Perform rhythmic patterns using motor skills and knowledge of music notation.

Game Description: *Rhythm Cat* (Figure 4.5) and *Rhythm Cat 2* are applications that function on iOS and Android devices, including iPads, tablets, iPhones, and other portable media players. Both programs contain the same game mechanics, which include playing along to a prerecorded track by tapping a touch pad in accordance with a specific rhythmic pattern. Early levels are organized by patterns with similar types of notes, with more advanced levels varying the patterns and even requiring the player to play with a combination of both hands. The accompanying songs are a variety of different styles and tempos, which grow more challenging as the levels progress.

Video Tutorial: See ▶ Video 4.5 on the OUP Companion Website.

Procedures
- 1:1 Device Environments
- Each student will begin with the first level and can progress through each level at the teacher's discretion. The teacher may wish to have students progress through the levels as a whole class or move at their own pace. The teacher may also wish to focus on a specific rhythm or a combination of rhythms, depending on the students' ability and the number of times the program has been used during class.
- 1:Multiple Device Environments
- Students can rotate in groups depending on the number of devices available and progress through different levels depending on the teacher's objectives. Teachers can check each student's scores at the conclusion of each level or have them play through each level at the same time.
- 1 Device Environments
- Teachers can project the device onto a projector, Smart Board, or Smart Panel with the proper adaptor and then can have students complete a level individually. An alternative method is to use body percussion or instruments to play along with the level while the teacher provides guidance.
- Remote Environments
- Students will need to download the application onto their portable devices if they have an iOS or Android device. As such, all students may not possess such devices and will not be able to use the game on their own. However, the teacher can share their screen and have the students complete the levels together by clapping if they are visible on the screen.

Adaptations
- Students who have physical difficulties in tapping the touchpad may need to perform with body percussion or instruments while accompanying the music.

- Students with auditory issues can use headphones to hear the music more accurately.

Assessments
- The game provides a scoring system based on how many notes were played correctly in the form of 0–3 stars. The game will allow students to progress to the next level if they attain a minimum score of two stars. However, the teacher may choose a specific level and require the student to receive a score based on their own method of evaluation.

Level Up!
- Teachers can have students create their own rhythms and have the class play along using body percussion or instruments.
- Students can learn the rhythmic notation of popular songs and play them using body percussion or instruments.

Limitations
- Students cannot save their work or submit it to a teacher. The teacher must watch the student perform each level in real time or check their scores before moving on to the next level.
- The game does not inform players of how to correct mistakes. Teachers must monitor students and work with them individually.
- For each note, the player must hold down the touchpad button for the entire duration. If the player takes their finger off too early, it will register as incorrect. This can be confusing as the game does not mention this important mechanical requirement.
- The free version only contains 15 levels. For additional levels, the teacher must purchase the full version for $4.99 per device.
- Players cannot alter the difficulty level or change the tempo of the individual levels.

Figure 4.5. *Rhythm Cat* by Melody Cats. Screenshot by the author.

Game Title: *Piano Dust Buster* and *Piano Dust Buster 2* by JoyTunes

Suggested Grade Levels: 3–6

Website: https://download.cnet.com/piano-dust-buster-by-joytunes/3000-20415_4-75834384.html?ex=RAMP-2070.0 (download link)

Objectives: Students will be able to:
- Perform various songs representing different historical eras, composers, and world cultures by playing on a virtual or real piano.
- Perform songs with melodic and rhythmic accuracy while receiving instant feedback through an embedded scoring system.

Game Description: *Piano Duster* and *Piano Dust Buster 2* (Figure 4.6) are rhythm action-type games that involve real keyboard playing through two options. The player can directly enter inputs on the iOS device using the touchscreen, or if the player has access to a piano, the player can use the device's internal microphone while playing. Players must touch the correct keys in rhythm with the prerecorded backing track to score points. A maid character moves around the keyboard while dust cartoons float down the screen toward a line where the player must tap in time with the music to "clean" them. Each correct input results in earning points; a final grade of 0–3 stars at the end of the song will determine if the player is allowed to progress to the next level. Players can also earn experience points by completing levels, allowing access to more songs. There are several levels in the starter pack at no cost representing various musical styles, composers, and eras of music history and culture. Additional songs require in-game purchases.

Video Tutorial: See ▶ Video 4.6 on the OUP Companion Website.

Procedures
- 1:1 Device Environments
    o Teachers will need to provide iOS devices, such as iPads, tablets, or other Smart devices to all students to play the game. Additionally, students can either tap directly on the touchpad or connect an adaptor from the device to an electric keyboard. The device's internal microphone can also detect nonelectric pianos, but multiple pianos playing together may disrupt the game. Students can work independently after receiving a tutorial from the teacher to complete selected levels. Teachers can also use the practice feature to allow students to acclimate to the gameplay.
- 1: Multiple Device Environments
    o Students can work in rotating stations on multiple iOS devices to complete levels and display to the teacher for assessment. Teachers can check each

student's scores at the conclusion of each level or have them play through each level without progressing until the teacher has given feedback.
- 1 Device Environments
    o Teachers can project the iOS device to a computer screen, Smart Board, or Smart Panel using an external adaptor. Students can either use the touchscreen on the teacher's iOS device individually or, if the teacher has access to a keyboard, the student can play using an internal or external microphone. If the teacher has access to multiple keyboards, students can play together. However, the game may not register multiple keyboards if they are not played together in rhythmic synchronization.
- Remote Environments
    o Students will need to download the application onto their portable devices if they have an iOS or Android device. As such, all students may not possess such devices and will not be able to use the game on their own. As such, remote options for this game may be limited without the ability for students to play along.

Adaptations
- Students who have physical difficulties in tapping the touchpad or keyboard may need to be evaluated individually as the tempo of the song cannot be slowed down.
- Students with auditory issues should connect their device to headphones to hear the music more accurately.

Assessments
- The game possesses an embedded numerical scoring system that increases when students play the correct note in the correct rhythm. At the conclusion of each level, players will receive a rating of 0–3 stars. A minimum of two stars is required to proceed to the next level; however, teachers may decide to use their own assessment methods in place of the game's scoring system to evaluate students.

Level Up!
- Teachers can use the different songs to further discuss elements of music, such as form, meter, melody, and harmony.
- Teachers can use a variety of songs to discuss stylistic influences, music history, composers, and world culture.

Limitations
- Students or teachers will need to create a login to save progress and scores. There is an option to proceed as a guest for quick play.
- There is no customizable difficulty, such as slowing down the tempo for novice players.

76　Gamifying the Music Classroom

Figure 4.6. *Piano Dust Buster 2* by JoyTunes. Screenshot by the author.

- Unlocking the full game requires in-game purchases. Sample levels are available for free.
- Students must play one level at a time to unlock new songs. If the students play on a teacher's device, the teacher may have already unlocked all sample songs and may choose which level the class should perform.
- Concert mode requires creating a free account to access.

Advanced Games

Game Title: *Bemuse: Beat Music Sequencer* by T. Pangsakulyanont and N. Suktarachan

Suggested Grade Levels: 5–8

Website: https://bemuse.ninja

Objectives: Students will be able to:
- Synchronize rhythmic patterns by using fine motor skills.
- Perform simple to complex rhythms in sequence with a variety of song styles.

Game Description: *Bemuse* (Figure 4.7) is a free, open-source website like rhythm action games such as *Guitar Hero* or *Friday Night Funkin'*. Rhythmic patterns represented by different colored bars travel down the screen toward a bar where players must input the correct key in time with the rhythm. Players' scores are determined by the fidelity of the inputs in terms of early, late, or on-time. Each song contains as many as five customizable difficulty levels in styles such as pop, jazz, soul, techno, house, and other genres. A large variety of songs are available, and they are constantly updated as new songs are written.

Video Tutorial: See ▶ Video 4.7 on the OUP Companion Website.

Procedures
- 1:1 Device Environments
  - Students can play the tutorial level to get acquainted with the program or the teacher can display the tutorial for the whole class. The teacher can pick the specific levels they wish the students to attempt or may allow the students to choose based on their level of experience with the game. Teachers can also determine the score and rating for student evaluation for each individual level. In addition, they may decide on the level of difficulty depending on the ability level of the student(s), or they may allow them to choose independently.
- 1: Multiple Device Environments
  - Students can rotate between devices in groups in combination with other activities. Students can share their scores with the teacher as part of a predetermined evaluation system designed by the teacher. Students can play for a certain amount of time before moving on to the next station.
- 1 Device Environments
  - The teacher can demonstrate a level using a Smart Board or a computer projector and then can invite individual students to the computer keyboard to complete a level. Students who are not participating can engage in other activities independently or in groups. This can be done in multiple lessons depending on the size of the class.
- Remote Environments
  - Students can play levels that are chosen by the teacher or that are independently selected. Students can share their screen or take a screenshot and share it with the teacher upon completing a level.

Adaptations
- Teachers can choose the difficulty level for students who need assistance or students with physical disabilities. The difficulty levels feature inputs depending on individual needs.

Assessments
- The game features an embedded scoring system that is based on the player's ability to successfully enter each beat on time. The score is displayed numerically in real time; at the conclusion of each level, the player is given a letter grade assessing their overall performance. Teachers can use these scores as a benchmark for their own evaluative purposes, or they can design their own methods of assessment based on their grading system.

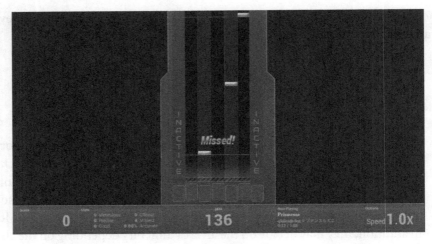

Figure 4.7. *Bemuse: Beat Music Sequencer* by T. Pangsakulyanont and N. Suktarachan. Screenshot by the author.

Level Up!
- The teacher can host competitions between individual students or teams of students.
- The teacher can use the styles of selected songs to segue into discussions of musical genres.

Limitations
- The game cannot be paused or stopped midway through the song.
- The background visuals and graphics can sometimes be distracting for some players.
- The songs cannot be slowed down for those students who need individual accommodation.

Game Title: *Note Fighter* **by MythicOwl**

Suggested Grade Levels: 5–8

Website: https://play.google.com/store/apps/details?id=net.notefighter.android&hl=en_US&gl=US
($1.99 download)

Objectives: Students will be able to:
- Identify pitches in traditional music notation by reading notes on the staff.
- Perform short pieces of music representing various styles and time periods using a virtual piano.

Game Description: *Note Fighter* (Figure 4.8) is a rhythm-action game that requires players to press the correct keys on a virtual piano while notes presented in traditional musical notation scroll across the screen. The player controls a steampunk-like character who strikes the notes when the player correctly plays them on the piano with the background music. If the player makes a certain number of mistakes based on the customized difficulty level, the level will end, and the player will be given the option to start again. A variety of songs representing different composers, time periods, and musical styles can be played. Songs are classified by level of difficulty, and players can play any of them in any order they wish.

Video Tutorial: See ▶ Video 4.8 on the OUP Companion Website.

Procedures:
- 1:1 Device Environments
  - Teachers can demonstrate a level or levels of *Note Fighter* for students before directing them to practice on their own devices. Teachers can have students choose the practice level before moving on to higher difficulty levels as they complete songs. Teachers can also have students select specific songs or can allow them to choose which song they would like to play based on their ability level. Teachers will need to circulate around the class and check each student to assess for completion.
- 1: Multiple Device Environments
  - Teachers can have groups of students play as part of a larger rotation of centers during the class. As students will have less time to play the game, the teacher may wish to assign specific songs or allow students to choose levels based on experience. Teachers will need to check each student individually for completion.
- 1 Device Environments
  - The teacher can project the game from an iOS or Android device onto a computer screen, Smart Board, or Smart Panel. Students will need to use the device individually to play, but other students can play along using classroom instruments if available.
- Remote Environments
  - Students will need to download the app separately, though the $1.99 cost may deter them. Therefore, a remote option for this game may not be viable, unless the teacher can project the game onto the screen and students have keyboard-type instruments to play remotely.

Adaptations
- The game rates each song as one to three levels of difficulty. Additionally, each song can be played in one of four difficulty levels: Practice, Artiste, Virtuoso, or Maestro. Players can commit more mistakes on the lower difficulties, while the higher difficulties eliminate the note names on the piano.

Figure 4.8. *Note Fighter* by MythicOwl. Screenshot by the author.

Assessments
- The game uses an embedded numerical scoring system for each note as they travel across the screen. Levels are either pass/fail and are labeled from one to three difficulty stars. Teachers can assess by requiring students to achieve a minimum score or simply completing the level or a series of levels.

Level Up!
- Teachers can use the songs in *Note Fighter* to discuss influential pieces, famous composers, song styles, musical form, eras of music history, and elements of music theory.
- Teachers can hold competitions to see which student can complete the most levels on each difficulty level.

Limitations:
- The game's title may be misleading, specifically in its negative connotation.
- Although notes are presented in traditional rhythmic form, performing the pitches in the correct rhythm is not a necessary requirement to pass each level.
- The app costs $1.99 per device and is only available on iOS and Android devices.

Game Title: *Vocal Match* **by Theta Music Trainer**

Suggested Grade Levels: 5–8

Website: https://trainer.thetamusic.com/en/content/html5-vocal-match

Objectives: Students will be able to:
- Match pitch vocally using diatonic and chromatic notes.
- Harmonize with different pitches vocally using diatonic and chromatic notes.

Game Description: *Vocal Match* (Figure 4.9) is a pitch-matching game that uses the device's microphone to register pitches produced vocally by the player. The game chooses different pitches that the player must vocally reproduce with a time limit that decreases with each level. Players do not need to sing in the same octave as the example pitch. Each round is scored according to how quickly the player can accurately sing the selected pitch for one second. In higher levels, the players must sing the pitch while harmonizing with other notes from an interval or chord.

Video Tutorial: See ▶ Video 4.9 on the OUP Companion Website.

Procedures
- 1:1 Device Environments
  o The teacher may conduct a vocal warm-up and have students complete a practice round to acclimate themselves to the sensitivity of the game's audio receiver. Once the students have sufficiently warmed up and completed a practice round, they may work independently to complete each level with or without teacher guidance. Students can show the teacher their scores at the end of the round or the overall level.
- 1: Multiple Device Environments
  o Students may work in groups or may rotate between devices in groups in combination with other activities. Students can share their scores with the teacher as part of the game's scoring system or a predetermined evaluation system designed by the teacher. Students can play for a certain amount of time before moving on to the next station, or they can work together as a choir.
- 1 Device Environments
  o Teachers may project the game on a Smart Board or computer and have the whole class sing together, individually, or in groups for each round. Teachers may also wish to use external microphones to record the whole class.
- Remote Environments
  o Students will need microphones on their devices to participate. If not, the teacher can have each student unmuted and play using the teacher's screen. If students have microphones, they can work independently and share their screen to show their scores at the end of each level.

Adaptations
- Teachers can have students compete against each other for the highest score.
- Students who excel can move on to more advanced levels that require vocal harmonization and interval training.

Assessments
- The game has an embedded scoring system based on how quickly the player can accurately sing each note in sequence. Points are accumulated based on how many rounds the player completes successfully and how quickly they pass each level. Teachers may wish to use their own assessment methods in place of the game's scoring system.

82 Gamifying the Music Classroom

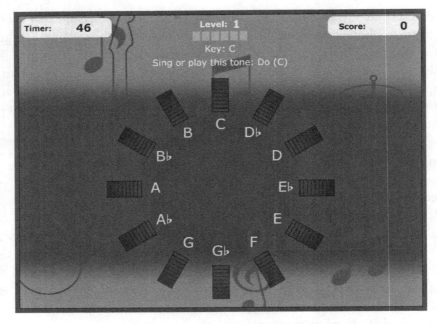

Figure 4.9. *Vocal Match* by Theta Music Trainer. Screenshot by the author.

Level Up!
- Teachers can use *Vocal Match* to discuss vocal range and technique, and they can give examples of musicians and performers.
- Teachers can use *Vocal Match* for interval training, sight-singing exercises, or pitch dictation.
- *Vocal Match* can be used as a segue to discuss vocal mechanics and biology.

Limitations
- Saving and logging scores require a login account, or teachers will need to check students' scores individually as they complete each level.
- Devices must contain a microphone to use the game effectively.
- Microphones may have trouble registering individual pitches if multiple students are using the program at the same time.

Game Title: *Pitchy Ninja* **by Pitchy Ninja**

Suggested Grade Levels: 5–8

Website: https://pitchy.ninja/

Objectives: Students will be able to:
- Vocalize single and multiple pitches diatonically, chromatically, and in intervals using prerecorded visual and audio prompts.

- Identify and perform diatonic intervals, scales, and arpeggios using vocalizations and solfege.

Game Description: *Pitchy Ninja* (Figure 4.10) is a side-scrolling, pitch-matching game that features several progressively difficult levels. Each stage focuses on the player reproducing a single note or group of notes in a predetermined rhythmic sequence. The game will play the target note preceded by two beats before each note. A level consists of 10 rounds that use random pitches each playthrough. Stages include pitch matching single tones, major and pentatonic scales, arpeggios, and harmonies, including major and minor thirds, perfect fourths, and perfect fifths.

Video Tutorial: See ▶ Video 4.10 on the OUP Companion Website.

Procedures
- 1:1 Device Environments
  o The teacher may conduct a vocal pitch-matching warm-up and have students complete the practice round to get acclimated to the sensitivity of the game's audio receiver. Once the students have sufficiently warmed up and completed a practice round, they may work independently to complete each level with or without teacher guidance. Students can show the teacher their scores at the end of the level to progress to the next level.
- 1: Multiple Device Environments
  o Students may work in groups or rotate between devices in groups in combination with other activities. Students can share their scores with the teacher as part of the game's scoring system or a predetermined evaluation system designed by the teacher. Students can play for a certain amount of time before moving on to the next station or work together as a choir.
- 1 Device Environments
  o Teachers may project the game on a Smart Board or computer and have the whole class sing together, individually, or in groups for each round. Teachers may also wish to use external microphones to record the whole class.
- Remote Environments
  o Students will need microphones on their devices to participate. If not, the teacher can have each student unmuted and play using the teacher's screen. If students have microphones, they can work independently and share their screen to show their scores at the end of each level.

Adaptations
- Teachers can have students compete against each other or teams for the highest score.
- Students who excel can move on to more advanced levels if they can attain the required score for advancement.

Assessments
- The game has an embedded scoring system based on how accurately the player can sing each note or group of notes in each round. Points are accumulated from the numerical score earned from each round out of 10 as a letter grade. A final letter grade is given from the average of each round at the end of the level. However, teachers may wish to use their own assessment methods in place of the game's scoring system if they can observe students directly.

Level Up!
- Teachers can use *Pitchy Ninja* to discuss vocal range and technique, and they can give examples of musicians and performers.
- Teachers can use *Pitchy Ninja* for interval training, sight-singing exercises, or pitch dictation.
- Pitchy Ninja can be used as a segue to discuss vocal mechanics and biology.

Limitations
- Devices must contain a microphone to use the game effectively.
- Microphones may have trouble registering individual pitches if multiple students are using the program at the same time.
- Students cannot save their progress or scores unless they create a free login account.
- Players must sing pitches in the octave in which they are presented. This may be difficult depending on the student's vocal range. The game's audio recorder is very precise; even a slight deviation from the presented pitch will result in a score deduction. Teachers should be mindful of this if they plan to use the game's embedded scoring system in their assessments.
- Players cannot progress to the next level unless they earn a score of "B" or better.
- The game does not inform the player which note or notes they are singing.

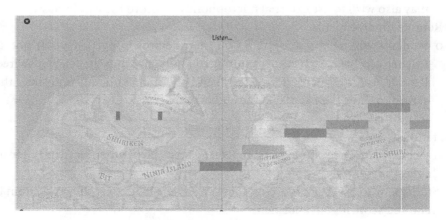

Figure 4.10. *Pitchy Ninja* by Pitchy Ninja. Screenshot by the author.

Summary

In this chapter, we discussed games that let players perform music in various capacities, from manipulating virtual instruments to using action-based performance simulators. Although the commercial genre of rhythm-action games may not have originally been designed for music-learning purposes, the elements of these game mechanics as evidenced by the games presented in this chapter can be used to not only effectively reinforce performance practice, but also to potentially increase motivation, engagements, and immersion. Chapter 5 will focus on games that promote mastery of musical concepts and how they can be used to help students understand, appreciate, and evaluate musical works.

5
Responding to Music With Games

Prelude

Understanding and analyzing the intricate elements of what makes music such a powerful and unique art form requires a deep knowledge of musical language and the skills to implement these concepts in performance. To a beginner, terms such as tempo, dynamics, timbre, and other musical jargon can be very confusing, especially when they are attempting to apply them in a practical context. Moreover, learning these concepts without applying them in hands-on activities can lessen the engagement and motivation of the learner.

Well-designed video games can achieve a balance between learning the analytical skills necessary to understand and operate complex systematic functions and expressing the individual creativity that is inherent to the performing arts (Miller, 2013). This balance is important in avoiding the "skill-and-drill" structure that relies on learning concepts through practicing a skill and repeating it endlessly without any variation or imagination. Used primarily for assessment purposes, this format has been referred to as "drill and kill" because of its tendency to bore students and kill any interest they may have in learning the material (Prensky, 2006).

While several of the games included in this chapter may appear to present a skill-and-drill structure, there are some key factors that differentiate them from the quiz-like format used so often in assessing growth. First, they offer progressive levels of difficulty, challenging students to do better when they achieve success in each task. Second, they give real-time quantitative assessment of progress, which leads to embedded rewards such as unlocking new levels and comparing high scores to other players. Third, students can customize their experience by choosing the level of difficulty suited to their abilities. And finally, the combination of graphics, gameplay, and immersion can engage students to participate for long periods of time.

I have used many of these games during my general music classes and have found that the competitive element is one of the most significant factors in keeping students engaged and in fostering the growth of learning musical concepts and skills. In many cases, students have asked to play these games just so they can improve their scores and outshine their peers. Students have frequently visited other students around the room just so they can see their scores and compare them, and even offer to help if they are having difficulty. They feel a great sense of pride and accomplishment when they beat their high score and can demonstrate their skills on a higher level.

It is important to monitor students so that their competitive nature does not become a negative attribute of the learning environment. Students who become too competitive can be easily frustrated when they are not achieving their desired goals, and sometimes they even leave the game out of anger, an action that gamers frequently refer to as "rage quitting." Using progressive and customizable levels of difficulty can maintain the quality of challenge while still having fun (Lazzaro, 2004). Overall, the games presented in this chapter can help students build skills in understanding, analyzing, and responding to how music creates meaning through its individual components.

Beginner Games

Game Title: *Pinkamusical Garden* by PBS Kids

Suggested Grade Levels: K–2

Website: https://pbskids.org/pinkalicious/games/pinkamusical-garden

Objectives: Students will be able to:
- Compose their own original musical patterns using various pitches and percussive sounds that represent different moods.
- Analyze and describe how musical sounds can be used in different emotional contexts.

Game Description: *Pinkamusical Garden* (Figure 5.1) is a game based on the show *Pinkalicious & Peterrific* on the PBS Kids network. Players can tap different pictures to hear musical instrument sounds and place them in one of three spaces that play a different pitch. Players can then choose one of the show's characters that is reflecting a different emotion, including happiness, sadness, anger, and silliness. Each emotion features a different set of musical sounds which the player can use in various combinations.

Video Tutorial: See ▶ Video 5.1 on the OUP Companion Website.

Procedures
- 1:1 Device Environments
  o Teachers can choose one of the character screens (happy, sad, angry, or silly) or allow students to choose independently. Students can then create their own music using the on-screen prompts and instrumental sounds. Once completed, teachers can have students play their work and explain how their music emphasizes the selected mood. If time allows, students can continue

creating music using other moods. Additionally, teachers can have students evaluate their own work and the compositions of their classmates using preselected criteria or rubrics.
- 1 Multiple Device Environments
  - Students can work in pairs or in rotating groups depending on the number of devices available. Students should have time to create one or more separate compositions and share them with the teacher, the group, or the entire class.
- 1 Device Environments
  - Students can take turns adding or removing sounds from an overall class composition as directed by the teacher. Teachers can decide on which mood to select, or they can use student choice. Students can also evaluate each composition based on how the music reflects the chosen emotion.
- Remote Environments
  - Students can work independently to create their own compositions as guided by the teacher. Either students or the teacher can choose the emotion at the teacher's discretion. Once completed, students can share their screen and play their compositions for the class. The class can also evaluate classmates' work using a predetermined rubric using musical terminology.

Adaptations
- Students who need additional assistance can work in pairs or groups. Students with sensory accommodations can use headphones as needed.

Assessments
- Teachers can set their own criteria for assessing students' ability to successfully create and play their own original compositions. Additionally, teachers can design their own rubrics to evaluate student responses to how their music reflects their chosen emotion and why the sounds used contribute to the overall musical experience.

Level Up!
- Teachers can use pitch placements to explore harmonies, such as dyads and triads.
- Teachers can use *Pinkamusical Garden* as a segue to analyze other pieces of music that reflect different emotional qualities.

Limitations
- The game does not allow the user to change rhythms.
- The game does not save students' music, so teachers will need to check students' work individually.

Responding to Music With Games   89

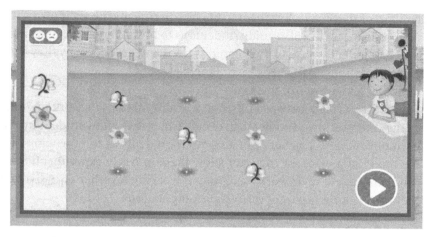

Figure 5.1. *Pinkamusical Garden* by PBS Kids. Screenshot by the author.

Game Title: *Melody Maker* by Google

Suggested Grade Levels: K–2

Website: https://musiclab.chromeexperiments.com/Melody-Maker

Objectives: Students will be able to:
- Create and edit original melodies using nontraditional musical notation.
- Understand and demonstrate the concept of tempo by manipulating an original melodic composition.

Game Description: *Melody Maker* (Figure 5.2), featured on Google Chrome, allows players to create their own melodies by clicking on a grid that plays a single pitch based on its position. To create harmony, players can click a button at the bottom of the screen that transfers the selected pitch to two spaces horizontally. Additionally, players can change the tempo from a metronome marking of 70 to 200. This can be edited while the music is playing or stopped.

Video Tutorial: See ▶ Video 5.2 on the OUP Companion Website.

Procedures
- 1:1 Device Environments
  o Students may work independently at their own pace after receiving a tutorial from the teacher. Teachers may wish to limit students to no harmony initially and eventually allow them to incorporate that feature with experience. Teachers may also direct students to implement a specific tempo or set of

tempos, or they may allow them to freely experiment with their own choice of tempo. Teachers can also guide students as to how tempo affects the mood of a piece. Students can play their compositions and describe why they choose a particular tempo to the class.

- 1: Multiple Device Environments
  - Students can rotate between different learning stations or work in groups to create compositions. Teachers can decide whether to allow students to use the harmony feature. Teachers can also guide students as to how tempo affects the mood of a piece. or they can allow them to freely experiment. Students can then present their work as a group if working together or individually if they are working as part of various learning stations.
- 1 Device Environments
  - Teachers can select students to come up to the board and select a note to place into the grid. Since the grid consists of eight horizontal spaces, teachers will most likely be able to create multiple compositions during one lesson. The teacher can also let the students select various tempos to play the piece and discuss how each tempo change affected the mood of the piece.
- Remote Environments
  - Students can work independently after receiving a tutorial from the teacher. Teachers can guide students individually if needed, or they can direct them to use specific functions of the program. After a period, students can play their compositions and describe why they choose a particular tempo to the class. Students can also evaluate their classmates' work using predetermined evaluation criteria or a rubric.

Adaptations

- Teachers can assist those students individually who are having difficulty understanding or manipulating the program. Students who demonstrate greater aptitude can also assist and collaborate with other students at the teacher's discretion.

Assessments

- Melody Maker does not provide an embedded assessment, for the program is used primarily for music composition with an emphasis on tempo alterations. Teachers can create a rubric that evaluates students' ability to complete a melody and experiment with various tempos, as well as their ability to describe and analyze how those tempos affect the emotional quality of the music.

Level Up!

- Teachers can use *Melody Maker* to transition into concepts involving changes in tempo.
- Teachers can segue into analyzing examples of music that illustrate different tempos.
- Teachers can use student compositions to introduce the concept of tempo as it relates to different types of emotional qualities.

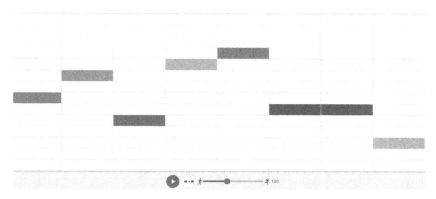

Figure 5.2. *Melody Maker* by Google. Screenshot by the author.

Limitations
- Students cannot change the rhythm, dynamic, or timbre of the melody.
- Students cannot save their melodies or share them online.

Game Title: *Musical Me!* by Duck Duck Moose

Suggested Grade Levels: K–2

Website: https://www.duckduckmoose.com/educational-iphone-itouch-apps-for-kids/musical-me/ (download on iStore or Google Play)

Objectives: Students will be able to:
- Perform and respond to musical activities, including playing songs, repeating musical patterns, and composing melodies.
- Analyze and describe the manipulation of musical content using genre-specific terminology.

Game Description: Students can choose from five separate mini games to create music and respond to musical activities. In the dance game, players can drag monster characters to different areas on the screen while they dance to different songs. The rhythm game requires players to tap on different birds as they scroll across the screen. The memory game is played by listening to notes produced by different planet icons that are played in different sequences and by reproducing the correct order. Players can create and play their own music with the notes game by choosing different songs and dragging notes up and down on the staff. Finally, the instrument game allows players to play different percussion instruments by tapping rhythms on their pictures (Figure 5.3).

Video Tutorial: See ▶ Video 5.3 on the OUP Companion Website.

Procedures
- 1:1 Device Environments
  o Teachers can choose which of the five activities students can play or allow them free exploration depending on time availability. Teachers can focus on one activity and have students share their work with the class in the dancing, notes, or instrument games. Teachers will need to check for understanding individually for the memory and rhythm games.
- 1: Multiple Device Environments
  o Students can freely explore the games in the time allotted or the teacher can have them focus on one game. Teachers can create a task to complete for each game or use the games to answer musical questions designed by the teacher. Depending on the number of devices available, students can work individually as part of rotating learning stations or in small groups.
- 1 Device Environments
  o The teacher can choose a specific game or group of games to present on the device, and then have students come up to play individually or in groups. The teacher can play the memory game with the entire class by asking which pattern is correct or by having students play along on body percussion or instruments for the dance, rhythm, notes, or instrument games.
- Remote Environments
  o The teacher can project the device using a screen share and use the format for a 1 device environment. Students will not be able to work independently unless all students have a separate iOS or portable device.

Adaptations
- Students can have the option to play any of the five games, depending on preference and ability level. The dance, notes, and instrument games are noncompetitive and can be played at the student's pace, while the memory and rhythm games offer more competition for advanced students.

Assessments
- There are no built-in assessments or scoring systems for any of the games. The memory game is the only game that offers a "correct/not correct" evaluation but does not score the player quantifiably. Teachers will need to develop their own evaluation system based on lesson objectives and predesigned rubrics.

Level Up!
- Teachers can use any of the games to segue to other musical concepts and activities. The rhythm, dance, and memory games can progress to activities to rhythmic performance, music theory, and physical movement. The notes and instrument games can be used to move forward to composition and performance using musical instruments.

Figure 5.3. *Musical Me!* by Duck Duck Goose. Screenshot by the author.

Limitations
- Players cannot save or share their progress. All evaluations must be done during gameplay individually.
- There is no scoring system or in-game evaluation.

Intermediate Games

Game Title: *Note Names* by Classics for Kids

Suggested Grade Levels: 3–5

Website: https://www.classicsforkids.com/music-games

Objectives: Students will be able to:
- Identify note names using the treble, bass, or alto clef.
- Spell basic words using note names on either the treble, bass, or alto clef.

Game Description: *Note Names* (Figure 5.4) has the player spell basic words by identifying notes made up of two, three, or more letters. There are 10 questions in a round; words are randomly generated per playthrough. The player can select notes with the treble, bass, or alto clef, but if they change clefs during a round, all previous progress will be lost, and the round will start over in the new clef. Each question gets progressively harder; students can try as many times as needed to complete a level.

Video Tutorial: See ▶ Video 5.4 on the OUP Companion Website.

Procedures
- 1:1 Device Environments
  - Teachers can work with students individually or allow them to work independently as each level is randomly generated. Students may also be able to work in groups on the same level. The teacher will need to circulate around the room and check for understanding. Teachers can also decide which clef setting the students will play or allow them to freely choose depending on experience.
- 1: Multiple Device Environments
  - Students may work in groups together or individually as part of rotating learning stations. Teachers can check to make sure the student has completed all 10 questions by viewing the completion screen at the end of the game. Teachers may need to provide resource materials such as worksheets that show notes on the staff with their corresponding names.
- 1 Device Environments
  - Teachers may select individuals to come up to the board to give the answer for each note name. Teachers may also group students in teams and have a competition as to which team can correctly answer the most questions in a round. Based on student experience, teachers may wish to use materials showing note names on their corresponding clef.
- Remote Environments
  - Students can complete rounds independently with or without teacher guidance. Teachers will need to check students' screens individually for evaluation. Teachers can also create their own words so that they can work with students as a whole class.

Adaptations
- Rounds are designed to increase in difficulty with each correct answer. Students who need additional assistance can replay earlier levels. Advanced students can design their own words and share them with other students.

Assessments
- The only embedded evidence of completion is at the end of the 10 questions. There is no scoring mechanism or recorded data of correct versus incorrect answers. Teachers will need to personally monitor each student for understanding and mastery.

Level Up!
- Teachers can use the words spelled in each question to reinforce concepts of vocabulary and language arts.
- Students can play the notes of each word by singing or using instruments.
- Students can create their own words using note names and sing or play the melodies on instruments.

Responding to Music With Games   95

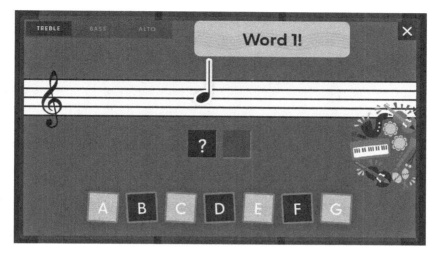

Figure 5.4. *Note Names* by Classics for Kids. Screenshot by the author.

Limitations
- There are no customizable difficulty levels. The game does not offer any assistance or tutorial beyond correct or incorrect answers.
- No sharp or flat notes are used in the game.
- There is no penalty or record for incorrect answers. Therefore, players can simply guess notes and choose the correct answer by process of elimination. Teachers will need to monitor student progress individually or develop an additional means of assessment.

Game Title: *Flashnote Derby* by Luke Bartolomeo

Suggested Grade Levels: 3–5

Website: https://flashnotederby.com/ ($2.99 download link)

Objectives: Students will be able to:

- Identify traditional pitch notation in either the treble, bass, alto, or tenor clefs.

Game Description: *Flashnote Derby* (Figure 5.5) is a racing-type game that requires players to identify pitches on the musical staff correctly to win a race against the computer system. Horses are displayed at the bottom of the screen, while notes appear at the top with a selection of pitch names. The player must choose the correct pitch before time runs out to advance and stay ahead of the computer. Scores are also displayed numerically based on the time taken to answer. At the end of each round, the player can see in real time if they have won the race and their final scores. If the player loses, they can review their incorrect answers and play again.

Video Tutorial: See ▶ Video 5.5 on the OUP Companion Website.

Procedures
- 1:1 Device Environments
  - Students may play independently based on their prior knowledge of pitch names, or the teacher may decide to use specific clefs and notes in earlier playthroughs. Students will be able to play several rounds in one lesson, so they may increase the number of questions and speed in the settings menu based on individual ability.
- 1: Multiple Device Environments
  - Students can work independently in small groups based on the number of devices available or as part of rotating learning centers. Teachers will need to individually check students' scores at the end of each round or have students show their work when completed.
- 1 Device Environments
  - The teacher can project the device onto a screen using an external adaptor. Students can call out answers when the teacher chooses them, or can come up to the board individually or in groups. The teacher can also separate the class into teams and have them compete against each other.
- Remote Environments
  - Students will need to have the game downloaded onto a personal device, such as an iPad, tablet, iOS, or Android. Since the game costs $2.99, a remote option may not be available for students to individually manipulate. However, the teacher may project the game onto their screens and have students write down their answers and post them in the group chat or show them on their screens.

Adaptations
- Several levels of difficulty are available, including settings for 10, 20, 30, or 40 questions in a round. Additionally, the speed at which the game progresses can be altered for beginner or advanced users, such as "walk" (slow), "trot" (medium), "canter" (fast), and "gallop" (very fast). Teachers and students can customize the number of notes on each clef used in a round, which includes treble, bass, alto, and tenor clefs. Instructional videos are also available to help students learn musical pitch as displayed in the treble or bass clefs.

Assessments
- Players receive a numerical score each time they enter a correct note, which increases depending on the time taken to answer. Each incorrect answer will result in the opponent horse gaining on the player's horse until it passes it. Teachers can either require the student to win a race on a specific difficulty level

Responding to Music With Games 97

Figure 5.5. *Flashnote Derby* by Luke Bartolomeo. Screenshot by the author.

at a predetermined speed customization or to receive a minimum number of points at the end of the round.

Level Up!
- Teachers can use instruments to have students play each note as it appears if the teacher is using one device and projecting it to the entire class.
- Teachers can create a competition setting based on the student who receives the highest score.

Limitations
- If they are working individually, students may need direction as to how to customize their difficulty settings. Additionally, students who are not monitored may customize their settings to their choices as opposed to the teacher's directions.

Game Title: *Staff Wars* by TMI Media, LLC

Suggested Grade Levels: 3–6

Website: https://apps.apple.com/us/app/staffwars/id810405576 ($.99 download for iOS or Android devices)

Objectives: Students will be able to:
- Identify traditional pitch notation in various combinations of clefs.

Game Description: *Staff War* (Figure 5.6), like *Flashnote Derby*, has players identify note names using customizable ranges and clefs. Like *Flashnote Derby*, too, players can choose the ranges of notes and which clefs they would like to practice. The notes move from the left side of the screen to the right; the player must identify them using the correct note name before they reach the clef on the left side. The player has three "lives"; identifying three incorrect notes will result in the end of the game. The game does not end until the player has used up all three of their lives. Even 10 correct answers will result in the notes speeding up and the game becoming more challenging.

Video Tutorial: See ▶ Video 5.6 on the OUP Companion Website.

Procedures
- 1:1 Device Environments
  o Students may play independently based on their prior knowledge of pitch names, or the teacher may decide to use specific clefs and notes and have students complete a game at the same time. Students will be able to play several games in one lesson, so they may attempt to increase their score, add notes to the range, or change clefs.
- 1: Multiple Device Environments
  o Students can work independently in small groups based on the number of devices available or as part of rotating learning centers. Teachers will need to check students' scores individually at the end of each round or will have students show their work when completed.
- 1 Device Environments
  o The teacher can project the device onto a screen using an external adaptor. Students can call out answers when the teacher chooses them or can come up to the board individually or in groups. The teacher can also separate the class into teams and have them compete against each other.
- Remote Environments
  o Students will need to have the game downloaded onto a personal device, such as an iPad, tablet, iOS, or Android. Since the game costs $0.99, a remote option may not be available for students to individually manipulate. However, the teacher may project the game onto their screens and have students write down their answers and post them in the group chat or show them on their screens.

Adaptations
- Advanced students can increase the range of notes or use different clefs, while beginner students can limit the range if necessary. However, customization of the note speed is not available. Notes can also be displayed as solfege if teachers

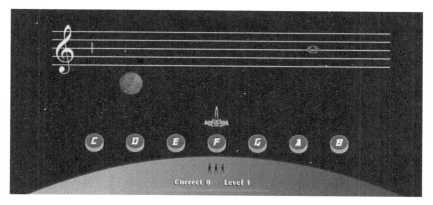

Figure 5.6. *Staff Wars* by TMI Media, LLC. Screenshot by the author.

prefer to use this method instead of alphabetical note names. The player can also customize the game to show the correct answer when a mistake is made.

Assessments
- Every correct answer adds to the overall score, which ends only when all three lives are lost. Teachers can require students to achieve a predetermined minimum score using a specific set of notes or range in one or multiple clefs. The game will save the player's highest score using that device.

Level Up!
- Teachers can use instruments to have students play each note as it appears if the teacher is using one device and projecting it to the entire class.
- Teachers can create a competition setting based on the student who receives the highest score.

Limitations
- There is no customizable difficulty level or method to change the speed of the notes.
- If working individually, students may need direction as to how to customize their difficulty settings. Additionally, students who are not monitored may customize their settings to their choices as opposed to the teacher's directions.
- Sharps and flat notes are not included.

Game Title: *Staff Dungeon* by Dr. Musik

Suggested Grade Levels: 3–6

Website: https://www.doctormusik.com/apps-and-games/staff-dungeon

Objectives: Students will be able to:

- Select notes represented on the treble clef by recognizing them on the staff.
- Choose correct notes on the staff to progress toward the game's exit.

Game Description: *Staff Dungeon* (Figure 5.7) is one of many games and activities available on the Dr. Musik website and the closest gameplay format to an adventure game. The game is a medieval-style fantasy in which the player controls a knight who moves on a grid by selecting from one of four note options on the treble clef. There are eight levels to complete, each getting progressively harder by adding obstacles in which the player must choose the correct note faster. The player has five "hearts"; hitting an obstacle or choosing incorrectly will cause loss of half a heart. When all hearts are gone, the game is over, and the player may try again. Players must choose the correct note to move toward a key, which is used to unlock the door to escape and clear the level. Players can also collect optional treasure chests, which are added to the overall score. Players are also scored by the number of moves they make before exiting the dungeon.

Video Tutorial: See ▶ Video 5.7 on the OUP Companion Website.

Procedures
- 1:1 Device Environments
    - Teachers will either need to review the notes on the treble clef or provide reference materials to students before playing the game. Teachers can have students work independently on each level consecutively or randomly based on ability. Students can display their scores to the teacher after completing a level. The teacher can then allow students to progress through each level as a quiz or review.
- 1: Multiple Device Environments
    - Students can work independently or in groups as part of rotating stations. Teachers will need to check student scores at the end of each level for assessment. Teachers can have students focus on a particular level or allow them to progress at their own pace based on ability.
- 1 Device Environments
    - Students can come up to the board individually or work in teams. Students can write down their answers while the teacher guides the class in the correct direction. Teachers can call individual students for answers for each move or take a poll from the class as to which note out of the four options is the correct answer.
- Remote Environments
    - Students may work independently or in breakout rooms to complete each level. Students will need to share their screen or take a screenshot and send it to the teacher to check for completion. The teacher can also share their screen and have students type in their answers in the chat box.

Adaptations
- There is no time limit to complete a level, so students can take as long as they need to choose the correct answer. Teachers can help students to determine the direction they should take to progress or can give them a multiple-choice option for each move.

Assessments
- Players are scored by the number of moves they make before completing the level. Teachers can use the numerical score in their evaluations or simply require students to complete specific levels. The score is displayed on the main menu but will reset completely if students exit the game. Players may start on any level they wish, but teachers may want to have students play linearly for a cumulative score.

Level Up!
- Teachers can hold competitions for "speed runs" or how long it takes for students to complete the level the fastest.
- Teachers can hold competitions for "no hit runs," or the ability to complete a level without making a mistake.

Limitations
- Sometimes the names of the notes displayed do not reflect their correct octave on the staff based on the surrounding note options.

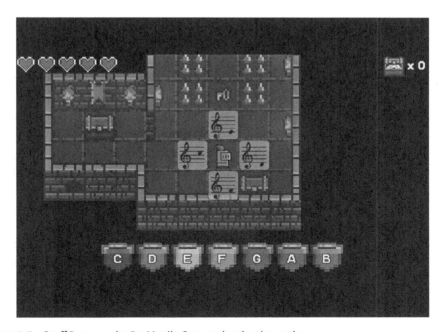

Figure 5.7. *Staff Dungeon* by Dr. Musik. Screenshot by the author.

- The notes can sometimes be difficult to see on the staff, depending on the size of the screen. A full screen option is available.
- Only notes on the treble clef are available, and the game does not offer any hints or assistance.

Game Title: *Instrument Match* by Music Teacher's Games

Suggested Grade Levels: 3–6

Website: http://musicteachersgames.com/instrument1

Objectives: Students will be able to:

- Use aural perception to identify musical instrument sounds.
- Associate pictures of musical instruments with their unique timbres.

Game Description: *Instrument Match* (Figure 5.8) plays different sounds representing instruments from the woodwind, brass, string, and percussion families. The player is given six choices with pictures of each instrument, while a single instrument plays a continuous melody. The player must choose which instrument corresponds to the sound being played. Each correct answer will earn points toward an overall score; incorrect answers will result in fewer points. The game can proceed indefinitely, though saving scores requires creating a free account on the Music Teacher's Games website.

Video Tutorial: See ▶ Video 5.8 on the OUP Companion Website.

Procedures
- 1:1 Device Environments
    o Students will need to have working knowledge of instruments, such as how they look and sound before playing. The game should be used as a review or an assessment of previously learned material. Students may work independently with or without teacher guidance once the teacher is confident of students' understanding of instrumental timbres. Teachers can have students play the game for a specific amount of time or can have them achieve a predetermined score.
- 1: Multiple Device Environments
- Students can work independently in small groups based on the number of devices available or as part of rotating learning centers. Teachers will need to individually check students' scores or evaluate students as they play to check for mastery.

- 1 Device Environments
  - Students can call out answers when the teacher chooses them, or they can come up to the board individually or in groups to select answers. Students can also write their answers down, though the teacher will need to check each one before moving to the next question. The teacher can also separate the class into teams and have them compete against each other.
- Remote Environments
  - Students can play the game on their own using a website link. They will need to project their screens so that the teacher can check for correct answers. Additionally, the teacher can play the game with the entire class and have them record their answers on the group chat or send them to the teacher directly.

Adaptations
- There is no customization for difficulty levels; however, there is no time limit to respond. Musical selections will continue until the player makes a choice. To be successful, students will need to have working knowledge of instrumental timbres before playing the game.

Assessments
- The game provides an embedded scoring system of numerical points when a player chooses the correct instrument. Teachers can either monitor students individually or play together as a group, depending on the number of devices available. Teachers may also direct students to achieve a specific score in a predetermined amount of time. It is recommended that teachers check students' answers, as questions will sometimes repeat, and the student may eventually choose the correct answer by guessing.

Level Up!
- Instrument Match can be used to expand on learning about different instruments, including their histories, construction, timbres, and playing styles.
- The instruments used in the game can be further showcased to highlight influential performers and significant compositions.

Limitations
- Students cannot save their scores unless they create a free account on the Music Teacher's Games website.

Figure 5.8. *Instrument Match* by Music Teacher's Games. Screenshot by the author.

- The game does not show players the correct answer when an incorrect selection is made.
- Players should use headphones if they are working independently, though it may hinder teachers' ability to assist.
- Questions tend to be repeated; students may eventually choose the correct answer by guessing.

Advanced Games

Game Title: *Channel Scramble* by Theta Music Trainer

Suggested Grade Levels: 5–8

Website: https://trainer.thetamusic.com/en/content/html5-channel-match

Objectives: Students will be able to:
- Use aural perception to differentiate between instruments of different timbres.
- Use aural perception to identify subtle changes in dynamic contrasts between different groups of instruments.

Game Description: Each level in *Channel Scramble* (Figure 5.9) uses a different set of instruments representing various musical genres played in a loop. Each instrument is represented by its name and picture below the mixer. During gameplay, each instrument's volume increases individually. The player must select which instrument's timbre is heightened and eventually clear all the instruments. Beginner levels use three instruments, while higher levels not only increase the number of instruments present but also heighten the subtlety of dynamic contrasts. Each level is also timed; correct answers that take less time to answer will earn more points. The level ends when the timer runs out or the player has completed all questions.

Video Tutorial: See ▶ Video 5.9 on the OUP Companion Website.

Procedures
- 1:1 Device Environments
- Students will need to have working knowledge of instruments, such as how they look and sound before playing. The game should be used as a review or an assessment of previously learned material. Students may work independently with or without teacher guidance once the teacher is confident of students' understanding of instrumental timbres. Teachers can have students play each level individually or can move forward together as a group. Teachers will need to check each student individually to record scores for assessment. Teachers can also have students' progress through each level at their own pace, but any progress above level 3 will require a free login.
- 1: Multiple Device Environments
  o Students can work independently in small groups based on the number of devices available or as part of rotating learning centers. Teachers will need to individually check students' scores or evaluate students as they play to check for mastery. The teacher can decide if students are to work on one or several levels depending on experience and mastery.
- 1 Device Environments
- Students can call out answers when the teacher chooses them or come up to the board individually or in groups to select. Students can also write their answers down, though the limited time allotted may make this difficult. The teacher can also separate the class into teams and have them compete against each other, but the teacher will need to choose the correct answer for the game to progress.
- Remote Environments
- Students can play the game on their own, using the website link. Students will need to project their screens or take a screenshot of their scores so that the teacher can assess completion. Additionally, the teacher can play the game with

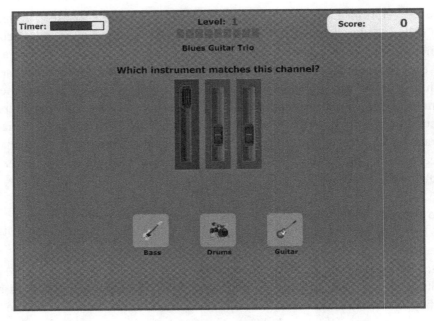

Figure 5.9. *Channel Scramble* by Theta Music Trainer. Screenshot by the author.

the entire class and have them record their answers on the group chat or send them to the teacher directly.

Adaptations
- Players can customize up to 20 levels from beginner to expert. Players can hear samples of each instrumental sound before playing, or they can use the practice option. Higher levels involve more instruments, different musical genres, and less contrast between dynamic changes between timbres.

Assessments
- Players receive a numerical score when answering. The amount of time it takes to answer will affect the number of points earned. The player receives a final score for each level when the timer runs out or all questions are answered. Teachers can set a minimum score for assessment or can require students to complete a level or multiple levels.

Level Up!
- The game can be used to expand upon learning about different instruments, including their histories, construction, timbres, and playing styles.
- The instruments used in the game can be further showcased to highlight specific musical genres and influential performers representing each style.

Limitations
- Students will need to create a free account to save their scores or progress past level 3. However, teachers can create a singular account and have students log in under the same information.
- The timer cannot be changed, and it depletes quickly.

Game Title: *Band Match* **by Theta Music Trainer**

Suggested Grade Levels: 5–8

Website: https://trainer.thetamusic.com/en/content/html5-band-match

Objectives: Students will be able to:

- Use aural perception to differentiate between instruments of different timbres.
- Use aural perception to identify different groups of instruments in performances of various musical genres.

Game Description: Like *Channel Scramble*, Theta Music Trainer's *Band Match* (Figure 5.10) is played by listening to a sound clip and choosing which instruments are playing out of a number of different choices. Each round has several questions that earn points upon correct completion. As levels increase, the number of instrument sounds, along with the number of answer choices, will increase as well. The game also features a timer that limits the amount of time players can spend on a level. A numerical score is given at the end of each level based on how quickly the player can complete all questions or when the timer runs out.

Video Tutorial: See ▶ Video 5.10 on the OUP Companion Website.

Procedures
- 1:1 Device Environments
- Students will need to have working knowledge of instruments, such as how they look and sound before playing. The game should be used as a review or an assessment of previously learned material. Students may work independently with or without teacher guidance once the teacher is confident of students' understanding of instrumental timbres. Teachers can have students play each level individually or move forward together as a group. Teachers will need to check each student individually to record scores for assessment. Teachers can also have students progress through each level at their own pace, but any progress above level 3 will require a free login.

- 1: Multiple Device Environments
  - Students can work independently in small groups based on the number of devices available or as part of rotating learning centers. Teachers will need to individually check students' scores or evaluate students as they play to check for mastery. The teacher can decide if students are to work on one or several levels, depending on experience and mastery.
- 1 Device Environments
- Students can call out answers when the teacher chooses them, or they can come up to the board individually or in groups to select an answer. Students can also write their answers down, though the limited time allotted may make this difficult. The teacher can also separate the class into teams and have them compete against each other, but the teacher will need to choose the correct answer to allow the game to progress.
- Remote Environments
- Students can play the game on their own using the website link. Students will need to project their screens or take a screenshot of their scores so that the teacher can assess completion. Additionally, the teacher can play the game with the entire class and have them record their answers on the group chat or send them to the teacher directly.

Adaptations
- Players can customize up to 20 levels from beginner to expert. Higher levels involve more instruments and different musical genres. For beginner students,

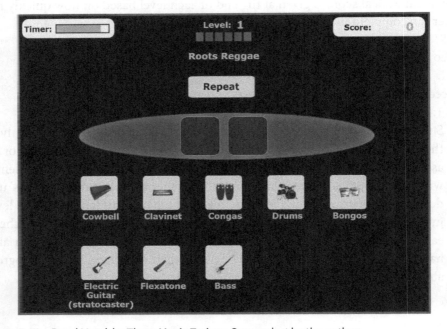

Figure 5.10. *Band Match* by Theta Music Trainer. Screenshot by the author.

teachers may assist by providing an answer for one of the instrument choices and by having the student choose the remaining sound.

Assessments
- Players receive a numerical score when answering. The amount of time it takes to answer will affect the number of points earned. The player receives a final score for each level when the timer runs out or all questions are answered. Teachers can set a minimum score for assessment or require students to complete a level or multiple levels.

Level Up!
- The game can be used to expand upon learning about different instruments, including their histories, construction, timbres, and playing styles.
- The instruments used in the game can be further showcased to highlight specific musical genres and influential performers representing each style.

Limitations
- Students will need to create a free account to save their scores or to progress past level 3. However, teachers can create a singular account and have students log in under the same information.
- The timer cannot be changed and it depletes quickly.

Game Title: *Tonic Finder* **by Theta Music Trainer**

Suggested Grade Levels: 6–8

Website: https://trainer.thetamusic.com/en/content/html5-tonic-finder

Objectives: Students will be able to:

- Use aural perception to recognize the tonic note of a song or scale.
- Identify note names on the piano to correctly choose the tonic note of a song or scale.

Game Description: *Tonic Finder* (Figure 5.11) is an aural training game that plays a variety of musical loops in a single key. The player can use a virtual keyboard to test out different notes before selecting which note in the music is the tonic, or "do." The player is given several answer choices at the bottom of the screen. Each correct answer will earn the player points; incorrect answers will remove them. There are six questions in each level; completing the level displays a final numerical score. Players have several "lives"; making a mistake will lose one life. Losing all their lives will end the game, but the player may try again. There is no time limit to complete a question.

Teachers will need to create a free login account on Theta Music Trainer to access any level beyond level 3.

Video Tutorial: See ▶ Video 5.11 on the OUP Companion Website.

Procedures
- 1:1 Device Environments
  - Students will need to have background knowledge of piano keys and scale structures, and preferably solfege training. The teacher should explain how the game works and demonstrate several questions before allowing students to work independently. Students should also use the practice feature if they are using it for the first time. Once the students are comfortable with the gameplay, they can work independently or in groups at the teacher's discretion. Teachers will need to check each student individually to record scores for assessment. Teachers can allow advanced students to progress to higher levels, while students who need additional assistance can repeat earlier levels.
- 1: Multiple Device Environments
  - Students can work independently or together in small groups based on the number of devices available or as part of rotating learning centers. Teachers will need to individually check students' scores or evaluate students as they play to check for mastery. The teacher can decide if students are to work on one or additional levels, depending on their scores.
- 1 Device Environments
  - Teachers can select students to answer questions or work together in teams. Students can also discuss and write their answers as there is no time limit. Teachers can spend as much time as necessary on each question. Teachers will also need to keep track of students' answers to check their progress.
- Remote Environments
  - Students can play the game on their own using the website link. They will need to project their screens or take a screenshot of their scores so that the teacher can assess completion. Additionally, the teacher can play the game with the entire class by projecting it onto the screen and have them record their answers on the group chat or send them to the teacher directly.

Adaptations
- Twenty levels can be chosen from without the need to complete earlier levels. Levels 1–5 require the player to find the tonic note using major tonality. Levels 6–10 change to minor tonality, while 11–20 allow the player to pick the tonic note out of different scales. More answer choices are given as levels increase. Teachers can choose the level or levels for individual students to practice or allow students to progress on their own after reaching a predetermined score. There is no time limit to complete questions, so students may work at their own

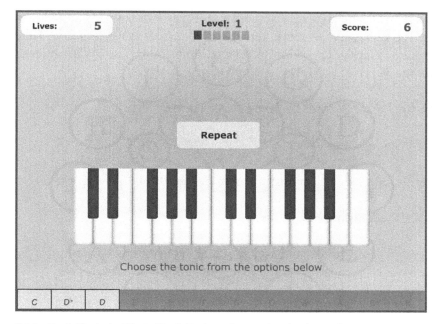

Figure 5.11. *Tonic Finder* by Theta Music Trainer. Screenshot by the author.

pace. The game also provides a practice mode to work on without losing lives if an incorrect answer is selected.

Assessments
- The game provides an embedded scoring system. Correct answers will earn the player points, while incorrect answers will take them away. Once the player has completed all questions correctly without losing all their lives, a final score will be displayed. Teachers can predetermine the score they feel represents appropriate mastery. Teachers can also set individual goals for students representing different ability levels or requiring additional assistance.

Level Up!
- Students can compete against each other or work together in teams to earn the highest score. The teacher can reward a prize to the highest scoring student or students.
- Teachers can use *Tonic Finder* to assist in aural training, practicing solfege, and differentiating instrumental timbre while determining the key and scale of a song.

Limitations
- A free account is required to access level 4 and beyond. Teachers can create an account and have students log in under the teacher's information.

- This is an advanced game that requires the player to have advanced knowledge of piano keys, scale structure, aural perception, and solfege training. Time limitations and lack of prior knowledge may limit students' ability to understand or play the game successfully.

Game Title: *Parrot Phrases* **by Theta Music Trainer**

Suggested Grade Levels: 6–8

Website: https://trainer.thetamusic.com/en/content/html5-parrot-phrases

Objectives: Students will be able to:

- Use aural perception to take melodic dictation from a series of musical phrases.
- Use a virtual keyboard or guitar to mirror various melodic phrases.

Game Description: *Parrot Phrases* (Figure 5.12) plays short melodic phrases that the player must repeat on a virtual keyboard. The player can also choose to enter notes on a virtual guitar fretboard, or if available, an electronic midi compatible keyboard can be used. Each level plays a short melody that must be repeated correctly to advance to the next question. There are several questions in a level. The game will end if the timer runs out, and the player will need to start over. Increasing levels become more difficult, requiring more notes to recognize and making less time available.

Video Tutorial: See ▶ Video 5.12 on the OUP Companion Website.

Procedures
- 1:1 Device Environments
- Students will need to have background knowledge of piano keys, scale structures, solfege training, and guitar tablature if they are to use the guitar option. The teacher will need to provide a tutorial and to demonstrate several questions before allowing students to work independently. Students should also use the practice feature if they are using it for the first time. Once the students are comfortable with the gameplay, they can work independently or in groups at the teacher's discretion. Teachers will need to check each student individually to record scores for assessment. Teachers can have advanced students progress to higher levels, while students who need additional assistance can repeat earlier levels.
- 1: Multiple Device Environments
- Students can work independently or together in small groups, based on the number of devices available or as part of rotating learning centers. Teachers will need to individually check students' scores or evaluate students as they play to

check for mastery. The teacher can decide if students are to work on one or additional levels, depending on their scores or progress.
- 1 Device Environments
    o Students can call out answers when the teacher chooses them, or they can come up to the board individually or in groups to select for each note or for an entire question. Students can also write their answers down, though the limited time allotted them may make this difficult. The teacher can also separate the class into teams and have them compete against each other, but the teacher will need to choose the correct answers for the game to progress.
- Remote Environments
    o Students can play the game on their own using the website link. They will need to project their screens or take a screenshot of their scores so that the teacher can assess completion. Additionally, the teacher can play the game with the entire class and have them record their answers on the group chat or send them to the teacher directly, though the limited time available may not make this effective.

Adaptations
- Players can choose up to 20 levels from beginner to expert or may use the practice option that eliminates the timer. Players can begin on any level they choose, regardless of past progress. Teachers can choose the level or levels for individual students to practice or to progress on their own after reaching a predetermined score.

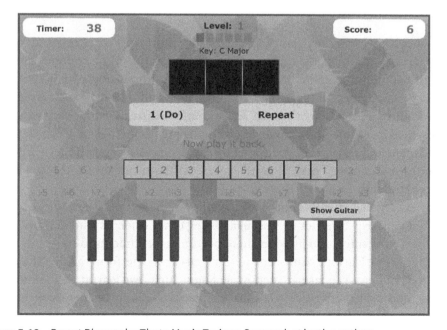

Figure 5.12. *Parrot Phrases* by Theta Music Trainer. Screenshot by the author.

Assessments
- Players earn points by entering the correct answer within the time limit for each level. Additional points are given for answering quickly, and points are not removed for incorrect answers. A final score is awarded when the player has completed all questions correctly or if the timer has run out. Teachers can use players' scores to evaluate their progress or develop their own assessment rubrics.

Level Up!
- Students can compete against each other or work together in teams to earn the highest score. The teacher can award a prize to the highest scoring student or students.
- Teachers can use *Parrot Phrases* to supplement aural training, practice solfege, and learn piano key placement and guitar tablature.

Limitations
- Players will need a working knowledge of piano keys or guitar tablature and aural perception, as well as an understanding of key and scale. Teachers will need to assess this knowledge prior to playing the game.
- A free account is required to access beyond level 3. Teachers can create an account and have students log in under the same information.
- Scores cannot be saved or shared without creating a free account.

Summary

In this chapter, we explored games that assist in training players to respond to a variety of musical prompts by applying terminology and aural perception. Through competition and other game-based elements such as immersion, interactivity, and focused practice, these tools avoid the traditional skill-and-drill test format that results from repetitive activities that lack variation. Instead, many of these games are presented in a game-show context that emphasizes excitement and fun. Teachers can find many ways to introduce competitive activities with games if they are careful to monitor students who may begin to experience frustration and jealousy of more advanced students.

In my experience, students not only have enjoyed the competitive nature of digital games but have expressed an interest in assisting other students who may be having difficulty. Competition also provides an opportunity for students to collaborate with each other, create learning teams, and in some cases even perform the role of teacher. In this way, students can take greater ownership of their own learning and ultimately become more self-motivated. The next chapter will reinforce these concepts by introducing games that relate artistic ideas to personal experiences through relevance and cultural contexts.

6

Connecting Musical Concepts With Games

Prelude

Music and related art forms provide natural bridges between areas of seemingly disparate subjects. Anchor Standards #10 and #11 of the National Core Arts promotes the connection of artistic ideas not only with material representing diverse cultures and learning constructs, but also with students' personal experiences to promote relevance and a deeper understanding of music's impact on the individual. Since playing games has been an integral part of human development since ancient times, integrating music with games can serve as an effective tool for realizing these goals.

Employing video games to explore various educational topics is by no means a new concept. Teachers as far back as the 1970s have used games such as *The Oregon Trail* (Rawitsch, Heinemann, & Dillenberger, 1971), *Math Blaster!* (Davidson and Associates, 1983)*, Where in the World Is Carmen Sandiego?* (Brøderbund Software, 1985), *Reader Rabbit* (Grimm, 1986), and Sid Meier's *Civilization* (Meier, 1991), to name a few (Criswell, 2009; deHaan, Reed, & Kuwada, 2010). Video games can help students experience learning in new ways that promote meaning and relevance by transforming identities through creating and experiencing video game worlds (Gee, 2005, 2007, 2013). Squire (2011) outlined several aspects of game design that can be used to foster connections between different areas of study, including employing academic knowledge as a tool for achieving goals, offering multiple ways of interaction so that players can solve problems, and embedding smooth transitions between information literacy and gameplay.

The other major aspect of the Connecting Standards is the importance of relating knowledge to personal experiences. Dewey (1938) stressed that students will be more motivated and successful if teachers link content to their students' personal experiences. Using digital resources based on content that reflects students' interests and popular culture has allowed the music curriculum to enhance college readiness, real-world connections, and the incorporation of technology to support what the National Standards refers to as "21st Century Skills" (Murillo, 2017).

21st Century Skills are the tools and abilities that students need to possess to be successful in college and to build a career. The advent of digital technology has made it possible to access a wealth of information, but this data is useless if it cannot be applied to real-world complex problems that require creative thinking and problem solving. This includes the ability to communicate effectively with others and to make decisions collaboratively to complete a shared objective. Developing these skills can result in higher job success, personal satisfaction, fulfillment, strengthened social connections, and a positive self-identity (McGonigal, 2011).

The games presented in this chapter represent potential ways for teachers to make connections with these skills through musical content. Among these connections are those with mathematics, language arts, social studies, science, technology, and social-emotional learning. Even more connections can likely be made with these games than the recommendations provided here. Teachers' imaginations and creativity are limitless when motivated to find new and exciting ways to spark student learning through relevance to their interests. As always, the lesson outlines are merely suggestions; teachers should feel free to modify or completely alter these plans to suit their own personal teaching style and the success of their students.

Beginner Games

Game Title: *Daniel Tiger: Feel the Music* by PBS Kids

Suggested Grade Levels: K–2

Website: https://pbskids.org/daniel/games/feel-the-music

Objectives: Students will be able to:
- Choose between different musical notes and sounds to create their own performance using visual aids.
- Connect musical content to different emotional states by choosing between happy, sad, and angry.

Game Description: The popular PBS Kids character Daniel Tiger serves as the main theme for this exploratory game (Figure 6.1). Players can choose one of three emotional states for Daniel, including happiness, sadness, or anger. The default setting is happiness, where different background music can be selected by clicking the musical symbols at the top of the screen. The player can then click a variety of pictures representing different musical notes and sound effects, which differ depending on the emotion the player chooses.

Video Tutorial: See ▶ Video 6.1 on the OUP Companion Website.

Procedures
- 1:1 Device Environments
    o Students can explore the game freely with limited guidance from the teacher unless the teacher prefers to focus on a specific emotion as a whole-class lesson. The teacher can either allow students to choose their own emotion and

create their own music independently or they can work together in groups focusing on one emotion at a time. Students can then perform their music for the class and describe why it reflects the emotion they have chosen or what the teacher assigned.
- 1: Multiple Device Environments
  o Students may rotate in learning stations, freely exploring the game or focusing on a specific emotion as assigned by the teacher. Students can create a performance of their work for the teacher, the group, or the whole class, and they can explain how their choices reflect the selected emotion.
- 1 Device Environments
  o Students can come up to the device individually or in groups to create their own performance, either selecting their own emotion or having the teacher assign one. Students can explain the choices they made to the class while the class offers their own comments in response.
- Remote Environments
  o Students can work independently or together in breakout rooms and share their screens when they are ready to perform. Students can use the chat feature to comment on classmates' work.

Adaptations
- Students who need extra assistance can work with others in learning teams, or students who demonstrate advanced ability can assist others who need help. The background music can be turned off for students with sensory issues. Students can also select a full-screen display to make images larger.

Assessments
- Teachers can assess completion of work through class participation, ability to create an original performance, and ability to describe how music can be used to express different emotional states verbally or in writing.

Level Up!
- The teacher can use *Daniel Tiger: Feel the Music* as an introduction to pieces of music that reflect a variety of emotional qualities.
- Students can connect to Language Arts standards by describing how music reflects certain emotions using writing prompts.

Limitations
- Students cannot save or share their work.
- Students can explore the entire game in a short period of time, so teachers will need to develop extra activities if they wish to use the game for an entire class session.

Figure 6.1. *Daniel Tiger: Feel the Music* by PBS Kids. Screenshot by the author.

Game Title: *Chrome Music Lab: Kandinsky* **by Google**

Suggested Grade Levels: K–2

Website: https://musiclab.chromeexperiments.com/Kandinsky/

Objectives: Students will be able to:
- Create original musical content using abstract visual art and geometric shapes.
- Compare painting to making music by turning artwork into sound.

Game Description: *Kandinsky* (Figure 6.2) was inspired by artist Wassily Kandinsky's philosophy that drawing and painting can be compared to making music. Google developed *Kandinsky* as a free web-based game whereby users can use the computer mouse to draw shapes, lines, and other objects on the screen. Players can click each drawing to hear an associated pitch, or they can select the "play" button to hear the combined sounds in melodic form. Players can also select up to three color schemes that change the instrumental timbre from a marimba to string instruments. The screens can be reset at any time to create new drawings, or the "undo" button can be selected to the right of the "play" button. Drawing geometric shapes will turn into different sounds, such as a circle that turns into a face which emits a vocalized pitch.

Video Tutorial: See ▶ Video 6.2 on the OUP Companion Website.

Procedures
- 1:1 Device Environments
  o Students may work independently or in groups after receiving a tutorial from the teacher. The teacher may allow students to freely explore or set guidelines

as to what shapes or range of pitches should be created. Students may then share their work with the class and have their classmates evaluate their music using a predesigned rubric.
- 1: Multiple Device Environments
  - Students can work in small groups as part of rotating learning stations. They may work either independently or together to create an original drawing. When complete, students can present their work to the teacher or the whole class. Students can also self-evaluate their work and have the class evaluate using predesigned rubrics.
- 1 Device Environments
  - Students can come up to the computer or board to create their own individual drawings or contribute to a drawing created by the whole class. This will depend on how much time is available in the lesson and how many students are present. Students can then self-evaluate their work and others by using predesigned rubrics.
- Remote Environments
  - Students can work independently or in breakout rooms after a tutorial from the teacher. The teacher may allow students to freely explore or set guidelines as to what shapes or range of pitches should be created. Students may then present their work to the class when completed by sharing their screen and have their classmates evaluate their music using a predesigned rubric.

Adaptations
- Students with sensory auditory sensitivities can use headphones or adjust the volume as needed. Students can also be given accommodation for any physical disabilities as per the nature of their classification.

Assessments
- Teachers can create objectives where students are required to create specific designs or allow them to draw freely. Students can share their work with the teacher, their group, or the entire class and self-evaluate using a predesigned rubric.

Level Up!
- Teachers can extend learning about the connection between visual art and music by playing works such as Mussorgsky's *Pictures at an Exhibition* or Dello Joio's *Scenes from the Louvre*.
- Teachers can connect music, art, and mathematics by encouraging students to create geometric shapes or specific designs that reflect mathematical concepts of symmetry, angles, or objects.

120   Gamifying the Music Classroom

Figure 6.2. *Chrome Music Lab: Kandinsky* by Google. Screenshot by the author.

Limitations
- Students cannot save or share their work.
- The player cannot control the tempo, dynamics, or any other aspect besides pitch.

Game Title: *Spectrogram* **by Google**

Suggested Grade Levels: K–2

Website: https://musiclab.chromeexperiments.com/Spectrogram

Objectives: Students will be able to:
- Produce and listen to musical and ambient sounds as displayed through spectrogram images.
- Understand how frequencies make up the quality of sound from low to high and how they change over time.

Game Description: *Spectrogram* (Figure 6.3) is available online through Google Chrome along with *Kandinsky* and other games mentioned in this text. Players can choose from a list of different sounds, including instruments, humans, and nature. When selected, each sound will play a prerecorded sequence that will be simultaneously displayed through the spectrogram. Players can also manipulate the spectrogram by using the microphone feature, which will convert their voice into an electronic sequence. They can also use the mouse or a touchscreen if either is available to create their own sequences. Audio mp3 files can be dragged onto the screen for an iconic representation of their sounds.

Video Tutorial: See ▶ Video 6.3 on the OUP Companion Website.

Procedures
- 1:1 Device Environments
  - The teacher can demonstrate how the spectrogram works by describing soundwaves and playing some of the prerecorded available sounds. Students can label which sounds are musical and which are nature or ambient sounds. Students then can create their own original spectrogram melodies by using the pointer tool. If the devices have microphones, students can use their voices, objects, or instruments to create a sequence. Students can then share their work with the class and have classmates comment on their work using a predesigned rubric or a listening map.
- 1: Multiple Device Environments
  - Students can play in sections as part of rotating learning stations. Students can work in groups individually or together to listen to and create their own sequences using either the pointer tool or microphone if available. When completed, students can share their sequence with the teacher and/or the entire class and have classmates evaluate their work. Students can also self-evaluate their work by describing how they created their sequence and what they observed when listening to classmates' sequences.
- 1 Device Environments
  - The teacher can cover the board so that the students cannot see the spectrogram and play the prerecorded sounds in random order. Students can then guess the sound and view their corresponding sequence. Depending on the class size, students can come up to the board and use either the pointer tool or the microphone to create a sequence one at a time or have students rotate in groups. When each student or group has completed a sequence, the class can describe what they hear using a predesigned rubric or a listening map.
- Remote Environments
  - The teacher can play the prerecorded sounds in random order without sharing the screen. Students can then guess the sound and view their corresponding sequence. Working independently, students can create their own original spectrogram melodies by using the pointer tool or microphone. After a set period, students can then share their work with the class and have classmates comment on their work using a predesigned rubric or a listening map or by posting in the chat section.

Adaptations
- Students should use headphones when possible to create their sequences and should adjust the volume as necessary for individuals with sensory audio classifications.

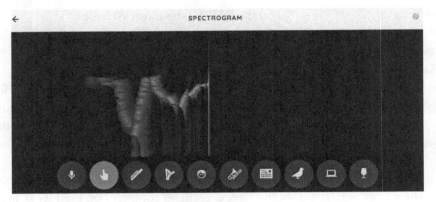

Figure 6.3. *Spectrogram* by Google. Screenshot by the author.

Assessments
- Teachers can create listening maps or rubrics that encourage critical listening by describing elements of each sequence. Students can use these materials to self-evaluate their own work or that of their classmates.

Level Up!
- Teachers can connect to science by discussing soundwaves and how vibration creates sound.
- Students can conduct a sound walk and describe sounds that they hear and how they are made.
- The teacher can play soundwaves of various sounds and have the students guess what sound it is.

Limitations
- Students cannot record, save, or share their original work.
- The additional sounds can only be listened to and not manipulated by the player.
- If a microphone is used in a large group or whole-class environment, the microphone may pick up the sounds of other students.

Game Title: *Paint with Music* **by Google Arts & Culture**

Suggested Grade Levels: K–2

Website: https://artsandculture.google.com/experiment/paint-with-music/YAGuJyDB-XbbWg?hl=en

Objectives: Students will be able to:
- Create and improvise music using different instruments by "painting" on the screen.
- Make connections between music and visual art using colors and shapes.

- Analyze musical ambience using different canvases representing various locations and art styles.

Game Description: Players can choose up to four different digital canvases representing various locations. Each location provides a different background ambience that is present during the brush movement. Several traditional instrument sounds are available, including flute, saxophone, trumpet, and violin, which can be "painted" on the screen by using the mouse or a touchscreen. Players can also toggle between a blank canvas and a heptatonic scale, which displays the names of the notes on the screen. The sounds play repeatedly in a constant loop, in which sounds can be removed or added. When completed, players can share their creations online through a weblink, email, social media, or Google Classroom.

Video Tutorial: See ▶ Video 6.4 on the OUP Companion Website.

Procedures
- 1:1 Device Environments
  o After giving students a tutorial on the game's mechanics, teachers can decide which of the four canvases to use, or they can allow students to choose their own. Students can select one or more instruments to paint on the screen. Teachers can direct students to use the "toggle notes" option to display note names or to keep the canvas blank. Teachers can also direct students to use specific instruments or note combinations or freely improvise. When completed, students can share a weblink with the teacher or post it in Google Classroom if available. Teachers can then play student work and have the class evaluate each piece using a predesigned rubric.
- 1: Multiple Device Environments
  o Students may work together in small groups or in teams as part of rotating stations. Teachers can have students freely improvise and provide feedback while observing or require students to choose instrumental combinations or a particular canvas. Students can self-evaluate or evaluate the work of classmates in their group using a predesigned rubric. Students can also play their work for the class as part of a group performance after submitting a link to the teacher or online classroom.
- 1 Device Environments
  o Teachers can have individual students come up to the board and paint sounds using a mouse or the touchscreen. Teachers can also have students work in groups, and each student can focus on one canvas. When complete, the teacher can post the link in the Google Classroom if available and have students evaluate the different sound paintings using a predesigned rubric.

- Remote Environments
  - Teachers can have students work independently or in breakout rooms to either freely compose or employ a set criteria as to which instrumental combinations on which canvas should be used. Students can post their link on the chat room or share it with the Google Classroom. The teacher can then play each student's work individually and have classmates evaluate each painting using a predesigned rubric.

Adaptations
- Students can use *Paint with Music* (Figure 6.4) with a mouse or a touchscreen if available, depending on student preference.

Assessments
- Teachers can evaluate students by either giving them specific tasks to complete or by allowing students to freely improvise and self-evaluate their work or the work of their classmates using predesigned rubrics. Since the program is primarily an exploratory game and does not possess any embedded assessment or predetermined objectives, teachers may decide how to evaluate student creativity from participation or by following specified directions.

Level Up!
- Students can use art supplies to paint their creations on canvas and play musical instruments or sing to explore how their artwork would sound if represented by music.
- Students can analyze works of art, such as paintings and sculptures, and imagine how they would sound if represented by music.

Limitations
- Players cannot control the rhythm or tempo of each instrumental melody.
- Players cannot change the notes of the displayed heptatonic scale.

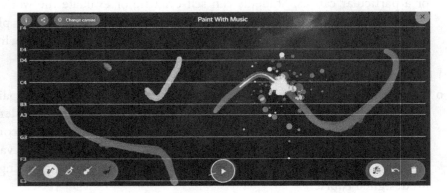

Figure 6.4. *Paint with Music* by Google Arts and Culture. Screenshot by the author.

Intermediate Games

Game Title: *Young Person's Guide to the Orchestra* by Carnegie Hall

Suggested Grade Levels: 3–5

Website: https://listeningadventures.carnegiehall.org/?ReturnUrl=%2Ftuba_game

Objectives: Students will be able to:
- Identify various instruments of the orchestra by aural and visual recognition.
- Learn facts about the orchestra by reading and analyzing informational text.

Game Description: Based on the Benjamin Britten classic piece, *Young Person's Guide to the Orchestra* (Figure 6.5) is an adventure game that puts the players in the shoes of a character named Violet. Violet receives a call from her Uncle Ollie, who tells her that she must go on a quest to find and rescue the instruments of the orchestra and bring them together to save the symphony. The journey takes her to different locations, where the player must identify each instrument's sound in several mini games. Players can read and reference each instrument family during the mini-games or access the map to choose which instrument game they would like to play next. When all the instrument mini games are completed, students will take a final quiz that can be submitted to the teacher if they are logged in.

Video Tutorial: See ▶ Video 6.5 on the OUP Companion Website.

Procedures
- 1:1 Device Environments
    - The teacher can begin the game as a whole class or can have students proceed individually. For first-time users, it may be better to work as a whole class until beginning the mini games, when teachers can decide if students should proceed linearly or use the safari map to select specific instruments. If teachers plan to use the game for multiple lessons, it may be easier to have students work at the same pace to better assess progress. Students do not need to complete every mini-game to access the ending; teachers can decide, based on the time available, which mini-game they would like their students to complete.
- 1: Multiple Device Environments
    - Teachers should introduce the game as part of a whole-class lesson, drawing close attention to how to access the informational text. When students are ready to complete the mini-games, teachers can have students work together in small groups or as part of rotating learning stations. Teachers will need to check student progress individually upon completing each assigned

mini-game, or they will have students play the game straight through to the end if time allows.
- 1 Device Environments
  o Teachers should proceed through the game linearly while pausing to read the informational text and defining vocabulary words. Students can work in small groups or teams or as part of a whole-class discussion to complete the mini games with teacher guidance. The teacher can decide which mini games to complete in order or selectively, based on available time. Teachers can also use multiple lessons to complete the game.
- Remote Environments
  o The teacher can go through the game by sharing their screen as part of a whole-class discussion. Students can also be placed in breakout rooms to complete mini games where teachers can access completion. Students who create a free login can save their work and resume playing in subsequent lessons.

Adaptations
- Teachers need to provide accommodation for students with reading difficulties because there are no customization options for font size or vocabulary. The character reads the text out loud, but teachers can mute the audio and have students read aloud either individually or in small groups. The mini games also do not allow for any customization, so teachers may need to individually assist students who are having difficulties.

Assessments
- Each game provides a different objective that relates to the overall story of reuniting the instruments with the symphony orchestra. Teachers can choose which mini-game or games they wish to use, and they can check students' progress as they complete the activities.

Level Up!
- Teachers can have students practice reading the informational text and define different vocabulary words.
- Teachers can use the game as a reinforcement to learn Benjamin Britten's *Young Person's Guide to the Orchestra* and other orchestral works.
- Several of the mini games are based on learning the different parts of instruments and how they function to make sound. Teachers can make connections to science by analyzing how instruments from different families work.

Limitations
- Using the "Local Game" option will not save the game if it is used in multiple sessions. Students must create a free account to save their progress.

Connecting Musical Concepts With Games 127

Figure 6.5. *Young Person's Guide to the Orchestra* by Carnegie Hall. Screenshot by the author.

- The full story can be a bit long for teachers who wish to complete the game in one lesson. However, teachers can have students play a specific mini game depending on the instrument chosen.
- The story references the concept of death several times, which can be uncomfortable for younger players.
- There is no customization for different ability levels.
- Games can be bypassed without receiving credit for completion.

Game Title: *Music Maps* **by Inside the Orchestra**

Suggested Grade Levels: 3–5

Website: https://insidetheorchestra.org/musical-games

Objectives: Students will be able to:
- Analyze the form and structure of musical works by completing a listening map representing different aspects, including instrumentation, dynamics, and tempo.
- Interpret visual representations of musical structure by listening and ordering musical events in the correct sequence.

Game Description: *Music Maps* (Figure 6.6) is a listening game that requires players to place blocks describing different sections of a musical piece in order. Each selection is approximately two minutes long and features different musical elements such as instrumentation, tempos, and dynamics. Players can pause or rewind the music if they need to hear it again before they make their choices. When the player believes that the order is correct, they can check by clicking "check my music map."

Video Tutorial: See ▶ Video 6.6 on the OUP Companion Website.

Procedures
- 1:1 Device Environments
    ○ Teachers can have students listen to the selection before playing the game. Students should have a working knowledge of musical terms such as tempo, dynamics, and instruments. If they do not, then teachers should review these concepts before allowing students to work independently. Teachers can either play the game with students as a whole-class lesson or circulate around the room assisting students as needed. When students have completed the first song, they can continue with the second selection with or without teacher guidance. Teachers will need to check individual students for completion.
- 1: Multiple Device Environments
    ○ Students can work in small groups as part of rotating learning stations. Teachers may wish to complete the first song with the entire class before having students work independently on the second selection. Students can either work individually or as part of a larger group using teamwork. Teachers will need to check students' screens to assess the completion of work.
- 1 Device Environments
    ○ The teacher can play each selection and have students draw the correct order individually or in teams. Teachers can then have individual students come up to the board and place each box in the correct order.
- Remote Environments
    ○ Teachers can proceed similarly to how teachers function in the 1:1 device lesson. Teachers can have students complete each selection individually or in breakout rooms as teams. Students will need to share their screens to show the teacher evidence of completion.

Adaptations
- Students can stop and rewind the piece so that they can listen to it as many times as needed. If the completed musical map is incorrect, the game will show a red outline around each box that is incorrect and a green outline for boxes that are in the correct places.

Assessments
- Students will receive a message indicating completion of each song. The teacher will need to check each student individually for completion. Teachers can also create additional listening maps for further assessment.

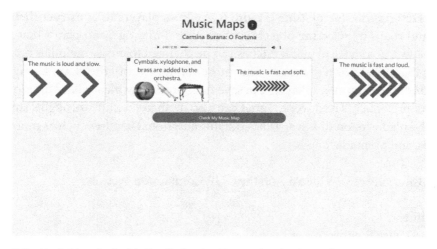

Figure 6.6. *Music Maps* by Inside the Orchestra. Screenshot by the author.

Level Up!
- Students can create their own music listening maps using selections provided by the teacher.
- Teachers can connect musical story maps to literacy and language arts by describing what is happening in the music.
- Teachers can extend learning by presenting examples of programmatic music that tells a definite story.

Limitations
- There are only two musical examples in the game, and they represent just traditional orchestral music.
- Students cannot save and share their completed work. The teacher will have to check each student individually for completion.

Game Title: *Isle of Tune* by Happylander Ltd.

Suggested Grade Levels: 3–6

Website: https://isleoftune.com/

Objectives: Students will be able to:
- Create their own original music using images representing different musical sounds and effects.
- Design their own cityscape using roads, trees, houses, and cars that animate with the music.

Game Description: *Isle of Tune* (Figure 6.7) allows players to construct their own cities and roads by selecting objects such as trees, buildings, and plants that play a sound effect or a musical pitch. Pitches can be changed to create melodies activated by cars that travel down the roads. The music continues until the player changes the roads or the environment. Players can save their tunes to work at a later time, or they can load previously saved work. Tunes can also be shared online through a sharable link. The iPad version of *Isle of Tune* contains additional features such as more cars, timbres, and premade loops.

Video Tutorial: See ▶ Video 6.7 on the OUP Companion Website.

Procedures
- 1:1 Device Environments
  - Students may work independently after receiving a tutorial from the teacher. Teachers may wish to conduct a practice session to familiarize students with each sound option and how to manipulate pitches to create tunes. Teachers can also provide short and simple exercises for beginner students before they are allowed to work on their own. Lessons can include focusing on a single option (trees, houses, etc.) or combinations to create ostinatos, canons, original melodies, or re-creations of existing songs. Students can then share their completed work by posting their link to a class forum and use predesigned rubrics to self-evaluate or evaluate classmates' work.
- 1: Multiple Device Environments
  - Students who are not familiar with *Isle of Tune* should be given a tutorial from the teacher before working independently. Teachers can provide specific guidelines as to how to construct musical material or whether to allow students to work freely on their own. Students can work individually in rotating learning environments or in small groups. When complete, students can post their link to the teacher or an online class forum and use predesigned rubrics to self-evaluate their work. When all groups have completed their tunes, students can evaluate each other's work.
- 1 Device Environments
  - Teachers can provide students with drawing materials and have them sketch out their road maps individually or in groups. Depending on the size of the class and the number of students, teachers can have students come up to the device individually or in groups to create their tune. When complete, students can post their link to the teacher or an online class forum and use predesigned rubrics to self-evaluate their work and the work of their classmates.
- Remote Environments
  - Students may work independently or in breakout rooms after receiving a tutorial from the teacher and practice time if they are inexperienced. Teachers

can provide specific guidelines and objectives as to the parameters of the tune, or they can allow students to create freely. When complete, students post their link in the chat box or the online class forum and they use an online predesigned rubric to self-evaluate their work. When all students have completed their tunes or the allotted time has elapsed, students can evaluate each other's work during class or for homework.

Adaptations
- Students who need additional time can save their work and complete it later. Teachers can make *Isle of Tune* a multi-part lesson to accommodate their students' time requirements.

Assessments
- Teachers can create a variety of tasks using *Isle of Tune*, such as creating loops using musical techniques and concepts (i.e., recreate a specific rhythm or melody, create an ostinato, or construct a musical scale). Assessments can also be completed through self-evaluative rubrics and rubrics evaluating the works of others.

Level Up!
- Connections can be made to architecture, geography, and spatial awareness. Students can create a thematic map or re-create a predetermined location.

Limitations
- The iPad version of *Isle of Tune* costs $2.99.

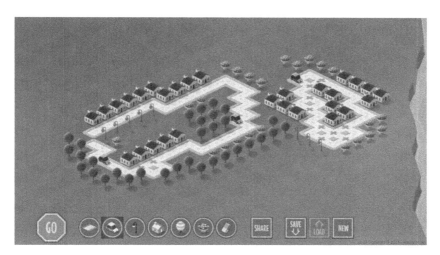

Figure 6.7. *Isle of Tune* by HappyLander Ltd. Screenshot by the author.

Game Title: *Beast Box* by Ben Mirin and the Cornell Lab of Ornithology

Suggested Grade Levels: 3–5

Website: https://academy.allaboutbirds.org/features/beastbox

Objectives: Students will be able to:

- Connect animal sound recordings with beatbox rhythms to create original music.
- Analyze the sounds of different wild animals and learn about their habitats.
- Improvise different combinations of wild animal sounds and beatbox rhythms.

Game Description: *Beast Box* (Figure 6.8) was produced in combination with Wildlife DJ Ben Mirin and Cornell University's Department of Ornithology. Players can create and mix their own music with recorded animal sounds with beatbox loopers. Animal species include elephants, whales, primates, birds, insects, and more. Players can choose from seven beatboxing background rhythms representing different ecosystems. The beatboxing rhythms are then matched with the player's choice of animal; up to five animals can be played simultaneously. Choosing five animals from the same ecosystem will unlock "Beast Mode," where players can click on each animal for different sounds.

Video Tutorial: See ▶ Video 6.8 on the OUP Companion Website.

Procedures
- 1:1 Device Environments
    o Students can experiment with different improvisation combinations after receiving a tutorial from the teacher. The teacher can allow students to freely explore different animal/beatbox combinations or can require students to choose animals from a specific ecosystem. Students can also match the sound of the animal with its name and attributes, or they can attempt to unlock the "Beast Mode" of each ecosystem. Teachers will need to evaluate students' work individually or have them work together in groups. Students can also self-evaluate or evaluate the work of classmates using predesigned rubrics.
- 1: Multiple Device Environments
    o Students may work together in small groups or in teams as part of rotating stations. Teachers can have students freely improvise and provide feedback while observing or require students to choose animals representing a specific ecosystem. Students can self-evaluate or evaluate the work of classmates in

their group using a predesigned rubric. Students can also play their work for the class as part of a group performance.
- 1 Device Environments
  - Teachers can have individual students come up to the board and add/edit sounds to the mix. Teachers can have students work as teams and focus on animals from a specific ecosystem, or they can have students compete to see which group can discover what five animals will unlock "Beast Mode." Teachers can also play the audio of each animal without letting students see which animal is playing, and they can have their students guess which animal is based on aural perception.
- Remote Environments
  - Teachers can have students work independently or in breakout rooms to either freely improvise beats or employ a set criteria as to which animal combinations should be used. Students can share their screen and play their mix for the class, and they can have their classmates evaluate each beat using predesigned rubrics. Teachers can also have students compete individually or in teams, revealing which group can unlock all the "Beast Mode" ecosystem beats first.

Adaptations
- All students, and especially students with auditory sensitivities, should work with headphones to prevent distractions. Students with specific needs can be allowed to freely improvise, or they can be monitored, depending on the nature of their classification.

Assessments
- Teachers can have students self-evaluate their work and the work of their classmates by using a predesigned rubric focused on improvisation. Teachers can also link assessment to science by using quizzes such as matching the animal to the vocal sound and matching animals to the same ecosystem. Teachers can also quiz students by choosing animals of different ecosystems or species.

Level Up!
- Teachers can use *Beast Box* to explore earth science and the biology of animals representing different genera and species.
- Teachers can have students analyze and compare the different sounds of animals within their own species group or from different classifications.

Limitations
- Students cannot record their own music or save it to share with others.
- "Beast Mode" is timed and will end automatically after a set period. When Beast Mode is activated, an additional track will be unlocked, and the player can freestyle mixing sounds with a bonus prerecorded track

Figure 6.8. *Beast Box* by Ben Mirin and the Cornell Lab of Ornithologys. Screenshot taken by the author.

Advanced Games

Game Title: *Perfect Pitch* by The Kennedy Center

Suggested Grade Levels: 5–8

Website: https://artsedge.kennedy-center.org/interactives/perfectpitch2/index.html

Objectives: Students will be able to:
- Analyze facts about different musical instruments representing different eras in music history.
- Create their own original musical sequences using their choices of instruments representing different musical eras.
- Test their knowledge of musical instruments in a baseball-style quiz format.

Game Description: *Perfect Pitch* (Figure 6.9) is a combination of mini-games and exploratory features made with a baseball theme. Instruments and musical periods are presented as the players of the game in the "Meet the Players" menu; players can view each instrument in four musical periods: Baroque, Classical, Romantic, and Modern. Each instrument has information about its construction, interesting facts, and its position in the orchestra. Players can choose the "Create a Lineup" menu to play their own musical sequence with different instruments. The "Play Ball" menu challenges players with a baseball-style quiz involving knowledge of instruments. Correct answers score runs in nine innings of questions; three levels of difficulty are available for increased difficulty.

Video Tutorial: See ▶ Video 6.9 on the OUP Companion Website.

Procedures
- 1:1 Device Environments
  - Teachers can begin by directing students to explore the "Meet the Players" section either independently, in groups, or as a whole class. Students can recite facts about each instrument to the class, or they can answer questions posed by the teacher. Students can also work independently with the "Create a Lineup" menu and share their compositions with a group or the class. When students have sufficiently explored these two menus, students can attempt the "Play Ball" quiz to test their knowledge. Teachers will need to check each student's scores for assessment; students can compete against each other for the highest score.
- 1: Multiple Device Environments
  - Teachers can have students explore the "Meet the Players" section and "Create a Lineup," or they can complete the "Play Ball" quiz, depending on the time available and the number of devices. This may take more than one session based on the number of students in the class. The teacher could also have students complete the quiz on their own after working with the first two games.
- 1 Device Environments
  - Students can take turns choosing which instruments to learn about as part of a whole-class lesson. For the "Create a Lineup" game, students can individually come up to the board and choose an instrument in the sequencer or work together in groups. The teacher can have students write down their answers to the quiz individually or work in teams as part of a competition for the "Play Ball" quiz. Several options to explore are offered, so multiple sessions may be required.
- Remote Environments
  - Students may explore each game on their own, or the teacher may prefer to guide students as a whole-class lesson. For the "Create a Lineup" game, students may work independently or in breakout rooms. Upon completion, students can share their sequence with the class and discuss it. Students can also complete the "Play Ball" quiz individually or in breakout rooms, but the teacher will need to have students share their screens to see their scores.

Adaptations
- Students can choose one of three levels of difficulty for the "Play Ball" quiz. Students can also raise or lower the volume of each menu as needed.

Assessments
- The "Meet the Players" section does not offer any embedded assessment. Teachers may create their own assessments using the information presented in the game. They can set guidelines for completion of musical sequences in the "Create a Lineup" menu. The most traditional assessment is available in the

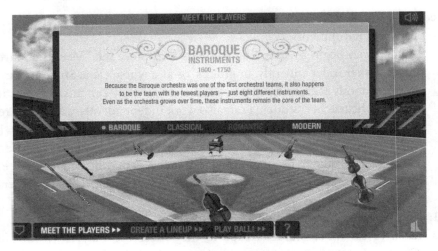

Figure 6.9. *Perfect Pitch* by The Kennedy Center. Screenshot by the author.

"Play Ball" feature. Students can complete the quiz using one of three levels of difficulty. Students will earn points based on how many guesses it takes to answer each question. Teachers can set a specific score for students to achieve to gauge understanding, but they will need to check each student's scores at the conclusion of the game.

Level Up!
- Teachers can connect playing music to other physical activities to promote health and science.
- Teachers can connect the act of playing music to learning about how the human body works, such as the skeletal system, the cardiovascular system, and the nervous system.

Limitations
- Students cannot save their work or share their scores online with the teacher.

Game Title: *Songlio* by Encore

Suggested Grade Levels: 5–8

Website: https://songl.io/quiz

Objectives: Students will be able to:
- Identify names of songs representing a diverse variety of musical genres using aural perception.
- Use their typing and spelling skills to quickly enter song names in a competitive-style single or multiplayer environment.

Game Description: *Songlio* (Figure 6.10) is a game show-style quiz that plays approximately 30 seconds of a song. Players must type in the name of the song using the hangman-style clues on the screen before the timer runs out. Points are earned for correct answers that are entered in the shortest amount of time. Players can select from pre-made games reflecting different genres of music, or they can select multi-player rounds where each player chooses a different song. Teachers can create their own quizzes with up to 10 songs, and they can send the link for students to play by themselves or multiplayer.

Video Tutorial: See ▶ Video 6.10 on the OUP Companion Website.

Procedures
- 1:1 Device Environments
  o *Songlio* can be used as a culminating activity or game show quiz after students study songs representing specific genres, cultures, or other identifying markers. Teachers can create their own quizzes of up to 10 questions using the *Songlio* library of over 4,000 songs. Students can log on to the multiplayer room and compete against each other, or they can work to achieve a minimum score decided on by the teacher.
- 1: Multiple Device Environments
  o Teachers can create their own quizzes and have students complete them individually as single players or in multiplayer rooms. Teachers can check the leaderboard to view students' completion and scores. Students can complete additional rounds based on the time available and the number of students in the classroom.
- 1 Device Environments
  o Students will need to write down their answers or be called upon by the teacher. The teacher can divide the class into teams and choose a different student to serve as a team representative for each question. Students can also design their own quizzes for classmates with teacher guidance.
- Remote Environments
  o Either the teacher or students can design quizzes to be completed as a single player or in breakout rooms as multiplayers. Teachers can check completion by having students share their screens or by viewing the leaderboard.

Adaptations
- Teachers can have students call out answers rather than typing them, if necessary. Teachers can also have students work together or in teams, and they can pick a representative to type or write the answer, depending on the number of devices available.

138 Gamifying the Music Classroom

Figure 6.10. *Songlio* by Encore. Screenshot by the author.

Assessments
- Teachers can view players' scores based on the number of songs answered correctly and the time taken to answer. Scores can be graded based on the teacher's method of assessment.

Level Up!
- The teacher can expand learning to include analysis of any songs used in the game, including a biography of the artist, the context of the time period in which the song was written, musical theory, and aesthetic viewpoints.

Limitations
- The game will not recognize answers that are not spelled correctly. However, it will leave a message stating "you are close" and will allow the player to continue if the spelling is almost correct.
- The game does not let creators choose what part of the song is played during the 30-second time interval.

Game Title: *BeepBox* by John Nesky

Suggested Grade Levels: 5–8

Web site: https://www.beepbox.co

Objectives: Students will be able to:
- Create and share their own original music using synthesized sounds representing chiptune music.
- Analyze and evaluate chiptune music examples from BeepBox and other 8-bit sources.

Game Description: Chiptune music as a genre first emerged in the 1980s with the advent of 8-bit video games with microchip-based audio hardware (Marquez, 2014). Gaming systems such as the Nintendo Gameboy were modified into programs that could create original compositions, such as *Little Sound Dj* and *Nanoloop*. *BeepBox* (Figure 6.11) expanded upon the four audio channels that were originally available in traditional 8-bit music into a free tool for creating music with synthesized instrumental and electronic sounds. The songs created in *BeepBox* can be saved and shared by posting a weblink. Many options can be customized, including meter, key, tempo, instrumentation, and audio channel. Instructions for simple and advanced editing settings can be found by scrolling down on the website.

Video Tutorial: See ▶ Video 6.11 on the OUP Companion Website.

Procedures
- 1:1 Device Environments
  o Teachers can give students specific tasks to complete as a tutorial for those with no experience with *Beepbox*. This can include working with one audio channel, a limited number of instrumental or electronic sounds, and a specific tempo or key. With more experience, students can begin experimenting with their own preferences based on learning objectives created by the teacher. When their compositions are completed, students can post them onto an online class forum or send them to the teacher directly. Students can use predesigned rubrics to self-evaluate their work or comment on their classmates' work.
- 1: Multiple Device Environments
  o Students will need to spend multiple sessions in small groups or in rotating learning centers to fully explore the various options offered by *BeepBox*. Each time a student works with *BeepBox*, they can be given more advanced objectives, such as increasing the number of audio channels, electronic sounds, and pitch variations. Students can also continue working on their compositions later by saving the weblink and returning to edit mode.
- 1 Device Environments
  o Students can come up to the board or device individually or work together in teams, depending on the time available and how many students are in the class. Because of the time needed to fully explore *BeepBox*'s capabilities, it may be necessary to have students work on their compositions at home if they have a device and internet connection. Teachers can also perform *BeepBox* compositions from other artists and have students evaluate them using predesigned rubrics.
- Remote Environments
  o Students can work on original *BeepBox* compositions on their own after receiving a tutorial and guidance from the teacher. If needed, the teacher can create breakout rooms for students who wish to work together or for students

140 Gamifying the Music Classroom

who need extra assistance. Students can post their links to the chat box, to an online class forum, or directly to the teacher. Teachers can then use predesigned rubrics to have students self-evaluate their work and/or evaluate their classmates' work.

Adaptations
- As *BeepBox* is an exploratory program, it does not have any customization settings for different ability levels. Teachers will need to provide guidance for those students who are having difficulty understanding how to operate the program. Students who show advanced ability with the program may assist other students, with the teacher's permission.

Assessments
- Teachers may create different objectives for achieving learning goals, such as creating music that utilizes different scale structures, keys, rhythms, tempos, and orchestration. All completed songs created by students can be saved and sent to the teacher via weblink. Teachers can also have students self-evaluate their work with a predesigned rubric and/or use rubrics to evaluate their classmates' compositions.

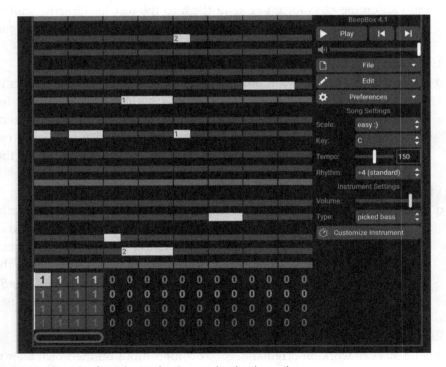

Figure 6.11. *BeepBox* by John Nesky. Screenshot by the author.

Level Up!
- *BeepBox* is a tool for students to learn about electronic music in the chiptune style. This can extend into exploring chiptune music from video games and contemporary chiptune musicians.
- Students can learn how music and science connect by discovering how soundwaves are expressed by 8-bit audio channels.

Limitations
- Use of *BeepBox* can be complicated for younger students and for those who have less experience with digital audio workstations. Teacher guidance and other tutorials may be necessary to explore the full range of options and capabilities.

Summary

Making connections to the world around us is one of the many opportunities that learning music can bring to all students. Combining this with digital game-based learning can add a new dimension to teaching that fosters engagement, relevance, and a link to the twenty-first-century skills that are increasingly needed for college and career readiness. The games presented in this chapter can help students understand relationships between math, language arts, writing, social studies, science, world cultures, and social-emotional learning.

The final chapter envisions what new advances are predicted to affect digital game-based learning and how it can be applied to music education. These predictions include innovations such as eLearning, massive multiplayer online games, and social media designed with education in mind. Emerging technologies such as adaptive learning machines, asynchronous learning, virtual reality, and artificial intelligence can be placed in the context of practical application to promote greater student engagement, collaboration, and immersion. As technology continues to evolve at a rapid pace, teachers must also adapt their practices to develop new ways to reach students. Embracing emerging game innovations could potentially influence how music education is taught in the future.

7
Future Directions

Prelude

One hallmark of technology is its ever-changing and evolving nature. By the time you read this book, there will most likely be many new gaming programs and applications to explore and play. As a result, technology can quickly become outdated and obsolete, rendering many previous texts dealing with the subject irrelevant. Unfortunately, there is no way to predict which websites or programs will be shut down, and I can only hope that the games featured in this book will stand the test of time. This may or may not be the case, however, as many digital programs that have been presented in other similar texts are no longer functioning. For example, Adobe Flash Player, a popular viewer for multimedia content, was discontinued in 2021, and as a result, many web applications were never updated and are not currently available.

The Covid-19 pandemic required many music educators to search out online and other e-learning resources to fulfill the learning requirements defined by state and national standards. Many teachers and students had different reactions to the massive redefinition of the classroom environment, but the necessity of learning online during the lockdown period led to a greater interest in these resources, an interest that has extended into the present (Rucsanda, Belibou, & Cazan, 2021). Although in-person learning has since returned to the school curriculum, digital tools have increased in both free and subscription-based services. We can likely assume that developers will continue to explore new opportunities for integrating digital game-based learning with music education. Since the states have mandated that technology be included in every subject area, the possibilities for incorporating video games in the music classroom are constantly growing.

Many of these innovations have begun to be or have already been implemented in both arts education and related subjects. Students' ability to connect with each other online through Massive Multiplayer Online (MMO) games has led to the development of new methods of communicating and sharing music with others all over the world. Augmented and virtual reality has transformed the educational landscape by blurring the lines between digital media and real life. Students can even create and modify their own games using free online websites such as Scratch and EarSketch. These technologies will most likely become more affordable and accessible as they are refined and used by increasing numbers of teachers.

To my knowledge, at the time of this writing no singular video game provides a comprehensive curriculum for general music or music appreciation classes. However, many design elements that are presently used in the games outlined in this book can be adapted to potentially create such a curriculum in the future. Using those elements, we can envision a game that would potentially assist teachers in developing students' musical knowledge and skills while simultaneously providing engagement, relevance, and enjoyment for which today's commercial video games are known. This advance has been accomplished through games ranging from *The Oregon Trail* to *Minecraft*. It is therefore reasonable to believe that a game designed for music education is not too far-fetched.

This final chapter envisions some of the current and possible future innovations that could affect the way music education is taught. From artificial intelligence to the creation of entire worlds dedicated to learning musical material, game developers are hard at work thinking of the next evolution in the digital revolution. However, it is only useful to discuss these advancements within the context of practice application, so we will focus on what has already been done and the next logical steps that will most likely follow.

Online Communities

Games that involve the ability of large groups of people to interact together in virtual worlds have been in use since the late 1970s. Early video game programmers such as Rob Trubshaw and Richard Bartle developed MUDs, or multi-user dungeons, whereby players could interact via text-based commands (Donovan, 2010). Even though graphics displays would not be available until years later, users were able to adopt a completely different persona to communicate and explore an entire fantasy world.

This experiment led to an entire genre of video games known as MMOs, which currently involve millions of players interacting daily. Participants can meet others, socialize, purchase goods and services, and even get married—all within the comfort of their own homes. The online world provides an affinity space, or a virtual location where people can come together around a shared interest or group of interests (O'Leary, 2020). Castronova's study of the online multiplayer game *Second Life* (Linden Lab, 2003) suggested that over 20% of frequent players considered interacting in the virtual world to be preferable to actual reality (Castronova, 2007).

Like *Second Life* and other popular games, including *The Sims Online* (Maxis, 2002) and *Palia* (Singularity 6, 2023), MMOs do not need to conform to the rules of games as a form of completing tasks and earning rewards. Instead, players can simply explore and connect with others at their leisure without having to worry about acquiring items or defeating difficult enemies to progress. For players who wish to experience cooperative challenges in a fantasy setting, another form of MMOs known as MMORPGs (Massive Multiplayer Online Role-Playing Games) have produced games such as *Ultima Online* (Origin Systems, 1997), *EverQuest* (Verant Interactive, 1999), and *World of Warcraft* (Blizzard Entertainment, 2004), among many others.

The success of MMOs and MMORPGs led educators to explore multiplayer online environments as vehicles to explore new avenues of student engagement and learning. Games designed specifically for education were shown to increase student engagement and collaborative action. After creating an MMO to be used by university students, Annetta (2006, 2008) concluded that the participants enjoyed learning through online multiplayer games because they wanted to be connected to each other, be entertained through multimedia, and have the ability to present their virtual alter egos and their work to others.

Sheldon (2012) noted that students exhibited greater motivation, teamwork, and a desire to create and problem-solve more than other digital game-based learning models that did not use multiplayer design strategies. As such, using gamification may create a greater sense of intrinsic motivation in students and provide them with life skills necessary to solve problems, work as a team, and think creatively. Teachers can create partner or group activities such as think/pair/share, round robin, or a roundtable discussion, all inside the virtual world (Childress & Braswell, 2006). This is reflected in MMORPGs such as *Adventure Academy* (Age of Learning, 2019), *Prodigy* (Prodigy Education, Inc., 2011), and *MinecraftEDU* (2016).

Online interactions through music making and performance have fostered what has been referred to as "sonic participatory cultures" (O'Leary & Tobias, 2017; Tobias, 2020). Sonic participatory cultures reflect the diverse ways that people engage with music and/or sound together through video games. Rewards for participating in these communities include social attraction to other like-minded individuals, a sense of group accomplishment, and a contribution to the development of the group. Examples include someone who makes and shares music within a video game world in an online community, which can occur individually or collectively.

Miller (2009, 2012) described collaborative music making in video game contexts as "schizophonic performances." Using games such as *Guitar Hero* and *Rock Band*, players can inhabit the persona of an alternate personality, even though they may not know how to play a real instrument. These games blur the line between reality and fantasy by combining the physical gestures of real performances with previously recorded sounds. Although players may be simply acting out a prerendered musical performance, rather than making something new and original, the enjoyment of playing comes from the act of creating new identities and from the immersion of gameplay.

Collaborative online music making is a feature of many MMO games. Participants can create and play music independently and with others as part of a group experience. The activities associated with the following games are offered not as essential for completing tasks, but as a way to socialize, perform, and explore all the opportunities the virtual world has to offer.

Final Fantasy XIV (Square Enix, 2013)—https://www.finalfantasyxiv.com
Available on Microsoft Windows, macOS, PlayStation 4, and PlayStation 5

Figure 7.1. *Final Fantasy XIV* screenshot. Image retrieved from Final Fantasy Wiki, "Patch 5.1 Notes," posted October 29, 2019. https://eu.finalfantasyxiv.com/lodestone/topics/detail/9356d16b030efd6e33a206087d811532980ef9cb.

To access the music-making feature, the player must activate the "Bard" class, which can be unlocked only after reaching Level 30. Attaining the Bard class requires the player to go on quests and complete challenges to receive experience points, which can increase the character's strength and other stats. Once the Bard class is available, an extra menu item called "Performance" will appear, and the player will be able to play virtual instruments.

Many instruments are available to play, mostly representing the Western European tradition. An extra feature that players can download is the Bard Music Player, which is available for free online. The Bard Music Player can play prerecorded music within the game if they are in Musical Instrument Digital Interface (MIDI) format. When one is ready to play, a keyboard will appear on the screen with a controller or keyboard buttons corresponding to the different notes. Players can change octaves by holding down a button or key while playing notes.

When the player has become proficient in manipulating the keys so that they play a melody or song, they can meet up with other online characters and spontaneously play together. There are no rewards for playing together or individually, nor does it contribute to completing the game. The music-making feature is an optional addition to the game, though it does require a significant amount of time to achieve the conditions necessary to play instruments.

Lord of the Rings Online (Standing Stone Games, 2007)—https://www.lotro.com
Available on Microsoft Windows, macOS

Characters immediately have access to playing instruments upon starting the game; additional instruments may be unlocked by purchasing from bards or learning

Figure 7.2. *Lord of the Rings Online* screenshot. Image retrieved from Chris Perry, "Play that funky music LOTRO," *PC Gamer*. December 13, 2011. https://www.pcgamer.com/play-that-funky-music-lotro.

from minstrels. The game has two kinds of musical production: freestyle, in which players strike keys on their computer to play individual notes, and ABC, which activates a precomposed sound file with a single text command. Geoff Scott, audio director, exclaimed that "we wanted [the music system] to be accessible to people. You don't want to be afraid of the music system if you're not a musician. We really encourage people to pick up an instrument and play around with it" (Cheng, 2014).

Individuals or groups of players can perform in locations derived from settings in the books, including the Prancing Pony Inn, the Shire, and Weathertop. Cheng (2014) conducted an extensive study on the music-making features of *The Lord of the Rings Online* to associate online virtual communities with creating and performing musical works. Anonymity could be a potential factor in building these communities, as there are no social expectations or real-world consequences.

ArcheAge (XL Games, 2014)—https://archeage.playkakaogames.com
Available on Microsoft Windows

Playing music in *ArcheAge* is based on acquiring materials to make music paper, which can be used to compose and perform songs. Music paper can also be purchased from merchants using in-game currency; players can hold up to one thousand music papers at a time. Creating a song on the music paper involves selecting pitches and rhythms by clicking on note names, note and rest lengths, dynamic, and tempo settings. There is a limit to how many notes the player can place on a music paper, but players can also make more notation paper if they have the materials.

Audio files are coded in a format called MML, which is uniquely created for the game and cannot be transferred to MIDI or any other universal file formats. Websites such as the ArcheAge MML Library feature songs created by other players that can be downloaded and copied into the game. Each time the player composes a song,

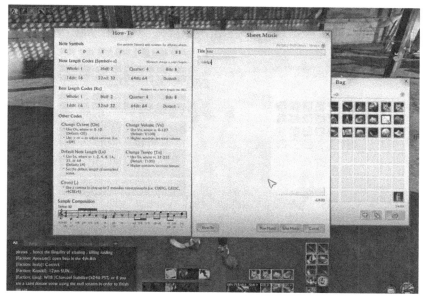

Figure 7.3. *ArcheAge* music player screenshot. Image retrieved from offroadguy56, "Archeage: Composing / Artistry Guide Part 1." YouTube video, 9:23. September 4, 2014. https://www.youtube.com/watch?app=desktop&v=5DeQ6Lctgas.

they will receive points toward the Composition skill. Acquiring a certain number of points will increase the player's proficiency, allowing them additional music paper and more musical material in each composition. This can be time-consuming, as higher skill levels require more points.

Sea of Thieves (Rare, 2018)—https://www.seaofthieves.com
Available on Microsoft Windows, Xbox One, Xbox Series X/S

Players can inhabit the persona of a buccaneer in this comedic take of the Golden Age of Piracy. Each character immediately has access to four instruments that represent the time period, including the concertina, hurdy-gurdy, drum, and banjo. Instruments can be customized with different color schemes and designs by spending in-game currency at equipment shops. The instruments can be selected from the main item menu and will automatically play one of several available sea shanties.

Players who form crews of up to four people can play together. The first person who begins to play will be designated as the primary melody, and all other performers will be automatically assigned accompaniment based on their instrument of choice. None of the shanties are historically accurate as they were either created for the game or adapted from traditional folk songs or popular culture such as the *Pirates of the Caribbean* film series. As with the other games, performing sea shanties individually or with others does not contribute to completing the game.

Figure 7.4. *Sea of Thieves* screenshot. Image retrieved from Sea of Thieves Wiki, "Instruments," posted by user Alianin. https://seaofthieves.fandom.com/wiki/Instruments

Though music-making features of MMOs, and MMORPGs can foster entire communities of sonic participatory cultures, at the time of this writing there is no known example of a game that involves an MMO construct for the objective of learning musical content or practicing musical skills. There may be several reasons why, such as the cost for individual or group licenses, the amount of servers needed to maintain large groups of online players, and the computer hardware necessary to support minimum data requirements to run the game. Additionally, using commercial MMORPGs in educational settings is difficult to monitor for content, as users are free to communicate with other players. This could lead to incidents of cyberbullying or inappropriate comments not suitable for a classroom environment.

Companies such as MusicEDU and Music First have developed comprehensive digital programs that involve online communications between teachers and students and are highly regulated. It is rational to consider the possibility that these companies or others will develop an MMO or MMORPG that can bring together large groups of people and that is based on educational objectives like games currently in operation that cover other academic subjects. Such a concept is feasible considering the increasing number of students who are gaining access to technology and the higher priorities that educational mandates are putting on its use in and out of the classroom.

Modding and Coding

Modifying, or "modding," is the act of altering a game's code to create new material from existing software. It includes the use of existing games to create new, stand-alone games, the use of software tools to change existing games by creating new content, or the use of other software to make games (Gee & Tran, 2016). It can be done with individuals or groups, and sharing mods among users is highly encouraged. Modders can also connect in social communities where they share ideas and learn from each other, often supporting each other's projects (O'Leary & Tobias, 2017).

While modding is the alteration of code from existing material to create a variation of the original software, coding is the act of creating computer software by programming instructions directly into the computer, such as algorithms and task assignments. Coding involves creating websites, applications, and other computer-based technologies using alphanumeric codes as a blueprint for performing functions. Over the decades, coding has evolved from a system of binary (0, 1) numeric codes to more user-friendly websites that assist the user and provide guidance for those who are not well versed in programming language.

Games have always been a source of both modding and coding, whether inherent in the game's design or by individuals creating new material based on the original source. For example, *Minecraft* allows users to freely create mods such as converting MIDI files into playable blocks that can be shared with different users. Other mainstream games such as the *Super Mario Maker* (Nintendo, 2015) and *Little Big Planet* (Media Molecule, 2008) series are specifically designed for players to create their own levels for others to play and review. Several of the games described in previous chapters were created using coding websites, such as GitHub, which was used to create the mods for *Mario Paint Sequencer* and *BeepBox*.

Other websites are designed specifically to code and create games, where users can work off a predesigned template or create a game from completely new code instructions. Websites such as Roblox, Stencyl, Flow Lab, Sploder, and Construct 2 all provide user-friendly instructions for beginners who have little to no coding experience. Completed games can then be uploaded to the website's server for other users to play and share. In some cases, however, these websites require in-game purchases to access other users' games. Roblox, for example, requires a premium membership to purchase in-game items using virtual currency called Robux. This had led to criticism that the developers deliberately limit their content moderation in order to market to minors (Parkin, 2022).

Since many commercial coding websites are not designed for classroom environments, alternative resources are available, with student learning as the focus for coding practice. Scratch and Scratch Jr. are popular websites for schools and are often used in computer and technology classes. Both websites help students to learn and refine coding techniques to create animations, add characters, and provide instructions to manipulate objects on the screen. Scratch and Scratch Jr. can be used to create rudimentary games but is primarily designed to help teach the basics of coding. Other websites that use the creation of games from an educational perspective as their main function include CodeCombat, GameSalad Creator, Gamestar Mechanic, and Gamefroot, just to name a few.

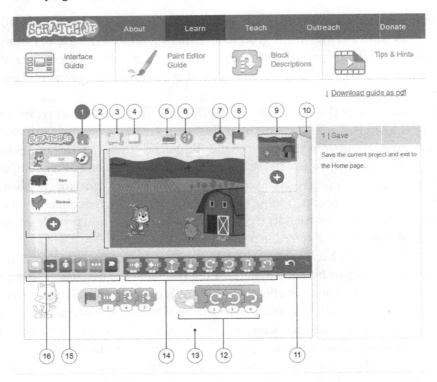

Figure 7.5. Scratch Jr. screenshot. Image retrieved from https://www.scratchjr.org/learn/interface.

Coding websites for music education can be like DAWs in that they can assign sounds in sequence to create musical material, but they differ by using coding prompts to create these sounds. For example, EarSketch uses text-based coding language to create and edit sounds, which are then placed in a DAW sequencer window for playback and mixing. Sonic Pi is a similar website but does not contain a sequencer window; instead, it displays music as soundwaves when played. These websites can be intimidating to those who are new to coding, as the inputs are advanced and require the use of tutorials. More education-friendly websites that can create music through coding and modding include Makey Makey, Playtron, and TouchMe, all of which transform objects such as fruits, play doh, and other conductive materials into MIDI controllers that can play sounds of virtual instruments.

Two excellent coding/modding websites that feature a combination of music and game creation are Blockly and Microsoft MakeCode. Blockly has several options, including making puzzles, mazes, and animations, and writing traditional music notation using coding prompts. Users can practice using a series of tutorials, each representing a more advanced function. For example, the first few levels concentrate on inputting note entries in a predetermined melodic sequence, while the later levels add more variations of rhythms, instruments, and harmonic structures. Once

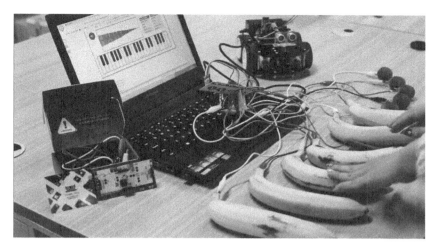

Figure 7.6. Makey Makey screenshot. Image retrieved from Kuongshun Electronic, "MakeyMakey Fruit Keypad Kit with Steps and Games." YouTube video, 1:38. April 3, 2019. https://www.youtube.com/watch?v=6i_rIzNuWLo.

completed, players can then create their own original music using coding prompts, and then upload to the Blockly gallery and share with other users.

Microsoft MakeCode combines games with music by providing an all-in-one coding/modding platform to create 1980s-style retro arcade games. Students can either modify existing games from the Microsoft library or create a new game entirely. Tutorials are provided for beginner users to input code and create characters, landscapes, animations, and gameplay controls. The music menu is embedded within the main creation menu and can be used to insert sounds or background music during play. Additionally, sound effects that play when an event occurs within the game or from player action can be combined simultaneously with the music.

Creations in MakeCode can be saved and published to the Microsoft server so that other users can view and play the games online. Since MakeCode is designed for kids, content is highly regulated; as a result, no inappropriate material can be created through the program. Use of both Blockly and MakeCode is free, and no downloads are required. Additionally, if the teacher has purchased *MinecraftEDU*, players can code projects that can be used in-game and shared among other players in MakeCode. Among the myriad number of coding and modding programs on the internet, Microsoft MakeCode and Blockly are the most accessible for making/performing music in a digital game-based learning environment. Any of these websites are effective for learning coding, but a relative few combine coding with the act of music production that are specifically designed for educational environments.

152 Gamifying the Music Classroom

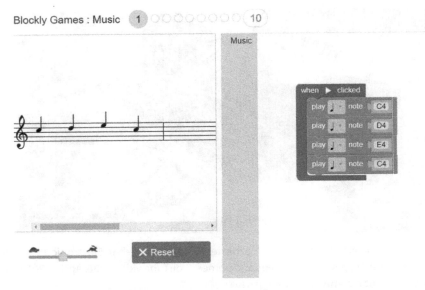

Figure 7.7. Blockly Music, screenshot taken by the author.

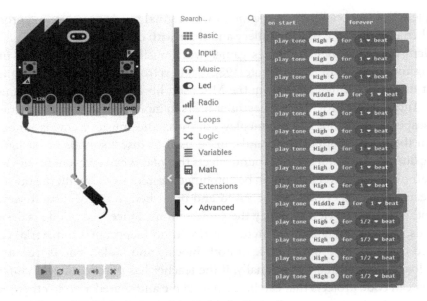

Figure 7.8. Microsoft MakeCode, screenshot taken by the author.

Augmented Reality

Augmented reality, also known as AR, enables visual prompts to be experienced in the real world through the medium of a device such as a Smartphone, tablet, iPad, or other portable media with a screen. This includes 3D modeling and display, which adds sounds and graphics to the look of an existing environment (Guclu, Kocer, &

Dundar, 2021). The term *augmented reality* was coined by Boeing researchers Tom Caudell and David Mizell in 1990, though the concept had been applied since 1968 when Ivan Sutherland and Bob Sproull developed a three-dimensional tracking system built into a headset nicknamed "The Sword of Damocles."

AR can be classified into three types, each defined by a different level of interactivity and technology integration. In Markerless AR, the device's camera can take a picture of a physical space and add digital images. This is present on nearly every portable device, including iPhones, iPads, Androids, or tablets that can add cartoon graphics or animations to a picture in apps such as Snapchat. Location-Based AR can take data recorded from the GPS system and use it to place objects in the real world through the visual interface. An excellent example of this applied to game-based technology is the popular game *Pokémon Go* (Niantic, 2016). During gameplay, players move around real physical spaces guided by their GPS system, which projects digital Pokémon onto the screen for players to catch. Finally, Projector-Based AR displays images onto specific objects using any Smart device (Clement, 2021).

Games such as the *Guitar Hero* or *Rock Band* series can be considered as augmented reality because of their use of peripheral controllers shaped like musical instruments. Though the controllers cannot play music outside of the context of the games, their inputs are registered on the screen and affect the game's outcome. However, these examples are not available on portable devices such as Smartphones or tablets, and they require a gaming console along with a visual interface (i.e., television or computer screen) to function (Kayali & Pichlmair, 2008).

Applications of AR to education have been documented as an effective supplement to traditional instruction and can be potentially more effective than textbooks or passive media watching (Cook, 2019). AR can also provide a contextual learning experience that combines problem solving with technology that subverts reality while doing so in real time. AR can encourage kinesthetic learning through hands-on participation, thus increasing student engagement and motivation (Diaz, Hincapié, & Moreno, 2015).

Music performance venues have taken advantage of AR technology in recent years, applying technology to concert experiences for greater immersion and promoting a more active listener experience. In 2019, the National Theater in London introduced "smart caption glasses," which display text and translations of lyrics in real time. Audiences viewing an opera performance, for example, can take a picture of themselves and download an app that allows them to virtually try on costumes and makeup (Clement, 2021). The nonprofit company Strings Music Festival offers a 360-degree AR virtual view of Strings Pavilion that makes the listener feel they are in the concert hall from the comfort of their home or any other location.

Some attempts to harness AR in the music classroom have led to several projects that are currently not available, such as a proposed glove to assist in learning music theory (Myllykoski, Tuuri, Viirret, & Louhivuori, 2015), a Smartphone app called "Prelude" for recognizing printed examples of notes and music symbols in the real world (Brown, 2014), an app called "Chord AR" for learning chord structures and

154 Gamifying the Music Classroom

progressions (Lu, Wang, Gong, & Liang, 2022), and an app from Singapore called "Playaralong" to help teach how to play drums through on-screen prompts displayed through a headset while playing a real drum set (Melnick, 2022).

More successful models that are at present available to consumers and educators are either stand-alone downloadable apps or features in larger curriculum packages. The AR Classroom which is provided as part of the MusicEDU Suite (https://www.musicedu.com.au) combines e-textbook information with portable media to reinforce musical concepts and skills. Using iPads or tablets, students can access the software suite through the login provided by the subscription service. After discussing a particular topic, students can travel around the room using their devices to play games and activities to practice skills. The MusicEDU Suite highlights games as a source of learning, frequently using video game characters, levels, challenges, and musical material to impart materials, including music theory, music technology, history, and other categories.

Figure 7.9. *Spatial Orchestra* (TCW, 2019), screenshot taken by the author.

The AR Classroom is only one feature of the MusicEDU software package, which must be purchased as a set in one annual subscription. There are also several stand-alone downloadable applications that incorporate AR technology into musical experiences. *Spatial Orchestra* (TCW, 2019) uses a Smartphone, tablet, or any other portable device's camera to project an image of the orchestra that responds to the user's movements. The user can walk around the virtual stage or project their own location onto the screen while listening to a selection of orchestral music. The app does not provide any instructional material or assessments, but teachers can use it to introduce students to the instruments of the orchestra in an innovative and interactive way.

Other AR apps mirror the style of rhythm action games, where shapes travel downward on the screen toward real piano keys that the player must play at the correct time. The embedded microphone in the device registers the timing of the keys and provides a score based on rhythmic and pitch accuracy. Examples of these games include *Magic Keys* by Dominik Hackl (2022), *Instant Musician* by Music Everywhere (2017), and *AR Piano* by AR Piano (2023). While all three games have the same concept of gameplay, *AR Piano* uses an Oculus Quest 2 headset as opposed to *Instant Musician* and *Magic Keys*, which uses the camera in a Smart device.

Potential hindrances of applying AR technology in the music classroom include the lack of available technology, such as acquiring portable devices for all students to access either individually or in groups. For students using Smartphones such as iPhones or Androids, it may be school or district policy that such devices be banned from use during instructional time, requiring the teacher to get special permission from an administrator to allow their use during class. Additionally, not all students may possess a Smartphone or other portable device, which could lead to feelings of shame or jealousy if other students do have one.

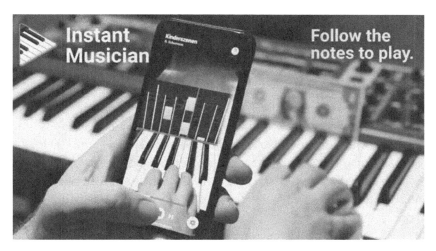

Figure 7.10. *Instant Musician* by Music Everywhere screenshot. Image retrieved from Music Everywhere, "Instant Musician Play Demo." YouTube video, 0:29. October 17, 2018. https://www.youtube.com/watch?v=wI6H06weTOg&t=21s.

Another consideration is the monetary cost of acquiring devices for each student. In many school settings, however, an iPad or tablet cart may be available to borrow, but the selected app would need to be downloaded on each device individually. Finally, since the stand-alone apps do not contain any lesson applications or embedded assessment, teachers will need to decide how they can work within their curriculum to fulfill predetermined learning objectives. These issues are even more present with virtual reality, a technology that fully immerses players into a completely digital environment but requires specific hardware and software to use.

Virtual Reality

Virtual reality, or VR, is different from augmented reality in that it completely immerses the user in a computer-generated world through a device such as a headset instead of just being viewed on a screen. In essence, AR supplements or enhances the real world, while VR completely replaces it through a completely 360-degree visual experience (Cook, 2019). Fully immersive VR uses sensors to track a player's body and position to place it directly inside a virtual environment, as opposed to simply interacting through a computer screen or overlaying digital components over real-world objects.

VR technology has been utilized by the military, educators, medical professionals, and private consumers since the 1960s. Games involving virtual reality first became popular in the 1990s, with its sophistication steadily increasing with each generation of hardware. This progression began in 2010 with the release of Oculus Rift's first portable headset, soon followed by HTC Vive and Sony's PlayStation VR in 2014. Virtual reality has been explored by influential technology companies including Google, Facebook, Samsung, and Microsoft for 3D visualization, communication, training, and creativity (Keeler, 2020; Mattoo, 2022).

Whether designed for gaming or any other additional purpose, VR technology requires specific equipment to be used properly. The main piece of equipment needed is the headset, which, depending on the system used, can be a standalone product or connected to an interface such as a computer or console. The PlayStation VR (PSVR) system, for example, is directly hooked up to a PlayStation system and cannot function without the console. Additionally, it needs a game CD loaded into the console to play, along with two battery-powered handheld controllers. Portable headsets, such as the Oculus Quest, HTC Vive, and Samsung Gear, can be connected to the internet; they contain memory for games to be downloaded and installed directly to the system.

Because VR technology has become more portable, accessible, and less expensive in the past few decades, developers have marketed virtual reality programs for educators as a full package, including the hardware and software for an entire class of students. Class VR provides specially designed headsets, along with teacher software, to regulate and post lesson materials for children ages 4–18. The programs available include virtual explorations of historical events, real-world locations, and scientific simulations. Additional suppliers of VR technology for schools include Lenovo, Robot Lab, and TD Synnex.

Concert venues and performing musicians have taken advantage of virtual reality to create new experiences for a wider audience. Instead of simply recording audio tracks or video performances, musicians have begun to digitally modify live performances for virtual reality hardware. Although the user does not have the ability to change or modify the performance in any way, the fully realized digital environment makes them feel as if they are actually in the concert hall watching a live performance. Joshua Bell recorded a live studio performance of Brahms's "Hungarian Dance No. 1" with pianist Sam Haywood for PSVR in 2017. The Symphony VR experience, launched in 2020 by the La Caixa Foundation, features Gustavo Dudamel with the Mahler Chamber Orchestra performing various influential works, and Music Up Close showcases the performances of the Chamber Music New Zealand string quartet.

Gaming remains one of the most popular uses for virtual reality equipment, including games designed with music as its core element. Music VR games are similar to the structure of rhythm action games, but they increase player immersion by displaying a 360-degree environment and a greater intensity of interaction. While games such as the *Guitar Hero* and *Rock Band* series represent augmented reality by its use of peripheral controllers shaped like actual instruments, VR furthers engagement by directly interacting with on-screen prompts. Games such as *Beat Saber* (Beat Games, 2019) use motion controllers to simulate beams of light that the player uses to cut through blocks in rhythm with the musical soundtrack.

Other music VR games include *Thumper* (Drool, 2016), where the player guides a beetle-like creature down a track by navigating it around curves and obstacles by pressing buttons in sequence with musical prompts. *Rez Infinite* (United Game Artists, 2015) is a combat-oriented game that requires the player to shoot lasers at objects with rhythmic accuracy. Harmonix, the creator of *Guitar Hero*, created a virtual reality version of *Rock Band* entitled *Rock Band VR* in 2016 that mirrors the gameplay of the original game. The player uses a peripheral controller in combination with the VR headset and can play along with various musical tracks in front of a digital audience.

Building on the success of these games and others, musicians and educators continued to develop new ways to practice musical skills through VR technology. Studies using VR to assist rehearsal practices, instrumental performance, composition, and conducting have all suggested that effective programs can not only increase engagement between students and teachers, but also assist in teaching these important skills (Bian, 2016; Chen, 2022; Pavlenko et al., 2022; Xiao, 2022). Below are some of the games showcased in these studies, in addition to games that promote common musical themes.

Figure 7.11. *Virtuoso VR,* screenshot image retrieved from https://virtuoso-vr.com.

Virtuoso VR (Really Interactive, 2020)—Available on Meta Quest, SteamVR, and Oculus Rift.

With *Virtuoso VR*, players can digitally explore and play several instruments, including drums, synthesizers, and other electronic sounds to create music in real time. Players can create loops or entire songs by interacting with the instruments on the screen using the hand controllers. The built-in microphone allows players to add vocals and effects such as reverb, tempo synchronizations, and distortions. When completed, songs can be uploaded and shared with the Virtuoso Community Library, and they are also available to other users to listen to or even edit. Songs can also be downloaded as mp3 or wav. files using the song exporter. Virtuoso costs $19.99 and is currently only available in English.

Music Inside (Reality Reflection, Inc., 2016)—Available on HTC Vive and Oculus Touch

Music Inside is a Korean VR game that allows users to play any song in real time with the use of the player's owned songs and Soundcloud. The player uses the motion controllers like drumsticks, striking a series of virtual drum pads in time with the music. A scoring system acts in combination with a timer to evaluate players' rhythmic accuracy. Players can choose from five levels of difficulty and can add customized drumsticks and background themes. Multiplayer mode is also available to play alongside friends or users anywhere around the world. *Music Inside* is available on the Steam store for $9.99.

Jam Studio VR (Jam Studio VR, 2020)—Available on HTC Vive, Oculus Quest, and SteamVR

Jam Studio VR, like *Virtuoso VR*, allows the player to freely explore and play different instruments, though in this case the instruments represent actual

Figure 7.12. *Music Inside*, screenshot image retrieved from https://www.oculus.com/experiences/rift/1357812410917539.

Figure 7.13. *Jam Studio VR,* screenshot image retrieved from https://jamstudiovr.com.

real-world equipment as opposed to digital synthesized creations. The instruments are preloaded with short melodies that can be accessed by touching them with the motion controllers. Players can customize their experience by selecting different musical genres, including orchestral, popular, and ethnic instruments. There is no scoring system; players are free to explore and play at their leisure. Players can also record their music and share it online with other users. *Jam Studio VR* has been used in music education classes, for special needs therapy, and for physical rehabilitation programs. It is available on the Steam store and Oculus Quest for $19.99.

Maestro VR (Symphonic Games, 2023)—Available on SteamVR and Meta Quest

Maestro VR is a new experience like *Fantasia: Music Evolved* in that it involves using the motion controllers to virtually conduct along with the music. Unlike

160   Gamifying the Music Classroom

Figure 7.14. *Maestro VR,* screenshot image retrieved from https://maestrovr.com.

Fantasia: Music Evolved, however, *Maestro VR* employs specific conductor rhythmic patterns to conduct a virtual orchestra using a variety of pieces representing various influential composers. Virtual environments include modern rehearsal halls, major concert venues, and even period representations such as the Baroque and Classical periods. Tutorials provide directions for right-hand beat structures and left-hand expressive motions, along with queuing specific instrumental and vocal sections. A "Masterclass" option is available, along with a virtual guide that assists the player in the basics of gameplay before attempting a performance. At the time of this writing, Symphonic Games, the creator of *Maestro VR*, is in the process of developing two music-themed games, including a game designed as a business simulation that allows players to run their own concert venue and an RPG-style game where a protagonist travels through a virtual kingdom to perform a concert for the king. *Maestro VR* is available on the Steam store for $29.99.

New games and programs are constantly being released, so it stands to reason that there will be many more music-themed VR games in the future. Music educators are already experimenting with VR to engage and provide a new and innovative form of learning for students. *Solstice VR*, developed by composer Roy Magnuson in 2018, is a compositional DAW tool that can help users create and share original music and is only available by request. Another program developed by Magnuson, *Ribbons VR*, like *Maestro VR*, is designed for players who wish to practice conducting technique, though currently it is only available for universities (Messina, 2021).

As promising as virtual reality technology is for its inclusion in music classrooms, several hindrances have prevented their widespread use at the present time. Users have sometimes experienced health issues during extended play, including digital fatigue, vertigo, exhaustion, and nausea (Mattoo, 2022). Additionally, while there are discounted prices specifically directed at schools, VR technology remains expensive, costing up to several thousand dollars for as few as 10 headsets. The headsets also require high processing power, vision compatibility, computer memory, and batteries, all of which may discourage teachers from making a financial commitment. Finally, since sharing music is not highly regulated, teachers may run the risk of violating copyright laws or having students access inappropriate or offensive material (Han, 2021).

Even with these potential issues, VR technology remains a highly popular emergent tool for educators in all types of classroom environments. It is reasonable to believe that VR developers will continue to make more affordable products and market them to schools and private consumers. Since virtual reality will most likely continue to grow in sophistication, its games and programs will become even more accessible to a large and diverse range of students.

Effective Game Design

At the time of this writing, there does not, to my knowledge, exist a video game that comprehensively addresses learning musical concepts and skills while providing the same immersion and enjoyment possessed by today's popular commercial games. That certainly does not mean that one will not exist in the future, as many game development companies are creating games that are blurring the lines between education and recreation. As discussed in this chapter, new technologies and the increased accessibility of gaming resources, along with the gradual understanding of the learning potential of video games in the classroom, are becoming more accepted in mainstream educational practices. This greater acceptance can also be attributed to the fact that more digital natives entering the teaching field grew up with video games as part of an established culture and so they understand and can manipulate the technology with ease.

As I mentioned in the beginning of this text, games are merely one tool in the toolbox for educators who have the interest and skills to implement them effectively. Each of the games outlined in the previous chapters performs a specific function and can be applied to learning musical concepts, practicing performance skills, creating and evaluating musical material, and connecting that material with other disciplinary fields. Many excellent music education companies now focus on supplying digital tools through a subscription-based service, such as MusicFirst, Quaver, and MusicEDU, to name a few, but unfortunately the lack of funding resources for many school music programs prevents teachers from acquiring these programs.

This is why this book has focused mainly on free, online resources that are easily accessible and are designed specifically with music education in mind. Teachers may wish to use commercially based games such as *Guitar Hero* and *Rock Band* in their lessons, but these games will be effective only if they fit naturally into a predesigned curriculum with learning objectives and built-in progress assessments. It is very important to consider the purpose of implementing games as lesson materials as opposed to simply including them because it may increase student engagement and motivation. While it is true that many people play games just because they are enjoyable, games should also activate higher cognitive functions such as memory, organizing information, and evaluating and solving problems (Denis & Jouvelot, 2005).

Games are designed for a multitude of reasons, but in line with their design for learning, they should achieve the goal of helping to make the player a proactive problem solver using critical thinking and creative assessment (Gee, 2013). They should satisfy the need for mastery of a given task, create competence through increasing difficult challenges, and provide relevant and immediate feedback to assess skill development (Annetta, 2010). Koster (2014) stated that successful games contain a range of challenges and player abilities, a variable feedback system, and opportunities to progress by learning from failure: "The holy grail of game system design is to make a game where the challenges are never ending, the skills required are varied, and the difficulty curve is perfect and adjusts itself to exactly our skill level" (p. 130).

Numerous attempts to create designs for educational video games have failed due to a lack of connection between a fun-playing environment and meeting educational objectives (Ibrahim, Vela, Rodríguez, Sánchez, & Zea, 2012). This failure may be attributed to the "skill-and-drill" format of quizzing players that can be simplified to regurgitating acquired knowledge instead of applying it to completing challenges and receiving rewards (Dondlinger, 2007). Successful video games are designed to make these goals compelling to players, but they also focus on the purposes of learning the content and the value placed on that knowledge (Squire, 2011).

Additionally, an appropriate level of challenge should be offered for players with differing skill levels. The difficulty should be just outside of the player's ability level to create an emotional investment, so that even if the player becomes frustrated, they will continue to play in order to complete tasks and achieve mastery (Lazzaro, 2004). The amount of investment within the game should also create a sense of immersion so that the player is completely involved in the game's narrative. Tasks should be followed with immediate and meaningful feedback, so that the player is not encouraged to try again but has learned from failure and will apply that knowledge in the next attempt.

Many game researchers and developers have outlined features of effective games that are designed for both entertainment and educational purposes. Here is a summary of those features that are present in games that accomplish both:

- Objectives presented as inherent to the game's system in a clear and relevant manner.
- A progressive system of challenges that reinforces the player's accumulated knowledge.
- Immediate and relevant feedback that informs the player of their progress.
- Customizable difficulty that forces the player to strive beyond their skill level.
- Embedded rewards that assist the player in completing the game.
- Opportunities to cooperate and collaborate with other players.

Good games for learning and fun employ all of these properties, even though the way they are presented varies greatly from game to game. There are myriad gaming genres, ranging from action/adventure, role-playing games (RPGs) to sports, puzzle, simulation, and exploration games, but certain common features of these games contribute to their enjoyment. These features could potentially be used in future titles geared toward learning music as their main focal point.

- Characters—Protagonists, antagonists, supportive cast members, and NPCs (non-player characters) all greatly contribute to a game's experience. Good games are populated with characters that the player can identify with and feel empathy for. In some games, the personalities and identities of the characters are already established, especially Mario (*Super Mario Bros.*), Sonic (*Sonic the Hedgehog*), Link (*The Legend of Zelda*), or Lara Croft (*Tomb Raider*). In many games, such as *Elden Ring*, the player has the ability to create their own character and customize their appearance as they see fit. Regardless, the main character serves as the player's avatar and gateway into the game.
- Narrative—Games have come a long way in establishing compelling storylines, from virtually having no plot aside from a basic premise (*Pac-Man*, *Space Invaders*) to stories that could easily be adapted into narrative form (*God of War*, *Horizon: Zero Dawn*). Many games have in fact been made from literary material, such as *The Witcher* series based on the books of Andrzej Sapkowski. Good stories draw in players and hold their interest, even when they are presented with difficult challenges and obstacles. Many contemporary games even have multiple endings based on the player's decisions or additional content, commonly known as side-quests, which are not required to complete the main game.
- World-Building—Whether in the Inkwell Isles (*Cuphead*), the Mushroom Kingdom (*Super Mario Bros.*), or the land of Hyrule (*The Legend of Zelda: Tears of the Kingdom*), creating worlds for players to explore has been essential to effective game design. In many cases, players can freely explore the game world without completing any tasks necessary to finish the game. The art style of the game world is also important to help immerse players in their surroundings. This does not mean that the graphics must be advanced; many popular games, like *Minecraft* and *Undertale*, rely on simple, even rudimentary graphics. These games are still influential because the environments themselves are steeped in the narrative and provide opportunities for the player to interact with characters, objects, and even other players.
- Gameplay—Nolan Bushnell, founder of Atari, has said that games should be "easy to play, but hard to master." Gameplay is a critical aspect of a game's success, particularly the game's mechanics as to how the player can manipulate their avatar. This could be as simple as the directions to *Pong*: "Avoid missing ball for high score" or pressing a specific combination of buttons to perform movesets and complicated actions. Gameplay also shows how the interaction of the player adapts to the environment. Games that possess technical issues or low

connectivity will lose a player's interest, regardless of the sophistication of the game's graphics or other attributes. Games that have been recognized for excellent gameplay include *The Elder Scrolls V: Skyrim*, *Hollow Knight*, and *Portal*.

- Sound/Music—A game's soundtrack can be lodged in the memories of players long after they turn off the game. From the earliest examples of chiptune music to today's fully realized symphonic orchestra recordings, melodies and character themes can define the tone of any game. The opening World 1-1 music from the original *Super Mario Bros.* has become iconic for even those who have never played the game, and live ensembles such as the Video Games Live Orchestra have performed game melodies in concerts all over the world. Sound effects are equally memorable, such as the four-note ascending chromatic theme from *The Legend of Zelda* whenever the player solves a puzzle or receives a critical item. Since the history of music is replete with examples of iconic music representing multiple styles and time periods, it will not be difficult to create a meaningful soundtrack that will help players immerse themselves in the gameplay.

- Collaboration—Since the time when the internet first allowed people to connect with each other from across the world or within the neighborhood, players have been collaborating and competing against each other in MMOs, MMORPGs, or multiplayer options outside of these genres. Many of these games have been discussed earlier in this chapter, but they can also include sports games, puzzle games, or games that offer temporary companionship. Games such as *Journey* and *Dark Souls* offer opportunities to cooperate with individuals without any text messaging or dialogue of any kind. Players can communicate with each other through gestures or sound effects to help each other defeat enemies, solve puzzles, or even just accompany them on their adventure. Working with others has become a major aspect of good game design, and even single-player games have websites and chat rooms where players can connect and help each other as part of a community.

- Relatability—Possibly the most important feature of a game is its ability to draw in players and make them feel they are part of the fictional universe. Though they may be just pixelated characters on a screen, players feel a real emotional catharsis for games that can connect with them on a deeper level. Scenes from games such as the *Final Fantasy* series, *Bioshock*, *The Last of Us*, and many others have made players cry, laugh out loud, jump in surprise, or feel an immense sense of joy and personal satisfaction. This connects to John Dewey's philosophy that to be effective, education should be relevant and meaningful to students. Games that can create meaning in players will be successful in creating a motivation pull to play, regardless of the context.

Summary

Digital game-based technology can enhance the music classroom in so many ways. New innovations are being created at an astounding rate, so it is likely that video game technology may one day be as ubiquitous as textbooks and sheet music. Based on happenings of the last few decades, the video game industry has only grown in influence in today's culture among people of all ages. Educators have already taken advantage of this expanding trend and have used new and emerging technology to design new experiences to provide an effective tool in the educator's toolbox. I personally am looking forward to when, not if, a game designed for educational purposes contains the same design features that make it comparable to the most popular commercial games to blend learning and entertainment. Perhaps one of this book's readers will help make that a reality, in which case, I am looking forward to playing it myself.

Epilogue

I first became interested in video games as a child, but I would never have imagined it would become my field of study as a doctoral student many decades later. For that, I must thank Dr. Hal Abeles, Dr. Kelly Parkes, and the other professors at Teachers College, Columbia University, for seeing the potential in the link between video games and music education. In addition, the works of many scholars, representing both music technology and the use of video games as a learning tool, were highly influential in creating this book.

Those who have studied the link between video game technology and learning and whose previous work on the topic has been indispensable include James Paul Gee, Kurt Squire, Marc Prensky, and Joey Lee. Music technology in education has advanced considerably through the efforts of Jim Frankel, Shawna Longo, Amy Burns, Bryan Powell, Marjorie LoPresti, Rick Dammers, and Steve Giddings, to name a few. Finally, those who have connected the bridge between these two disciplines are continuing to make great strides in furthering the cause of video games in music education; these include Jared O'Leary, Evan Tobias, Tim Summers, and Ethan Hein. Any serious educator or potential educator who wishes to gain more knowledge about the topics covered in this book would be wise to become familiar with all of these individuals.

It is my hope that this book has in some small way contributed to the field of music education. If you have found even one of these concepts or games mentioned to be interesting and worth further attention, then I feel that this book has served its purpose. The most important thing to remember is that everyone has their own personal teaching style. Using video games to achieve learning objectives can only be successful in the hands of a teacher who makes it their own. I invite you to alter any of the lesson plans, discover new games, and use your own judgment to decide what will work best for your students. Another important thing that the future of music and video games has in common is that the only limit is our imagination. So good luck, have fun, and game on!

APPENDIX
List of Games

Game Title	Developer	OS	Concept	Standard	Level
Band Match	Theta Music	Online	Timbre Recognition	Responding	Advanced
Beast Box	Ben Mirin and The Cornell Lab	Online	Rhythmic Composition	Connecting	Intermediate
Beep Box	John Nesky	Online	Composition	Connecting	Advanced
Bemuse: Beat Sequencer	Bemuse	Online	Rhythm Performance	Performing	Advanced
Carmen's World Orchestra	PBS Kids	Online	Play Instrument Sounds	Performing	Beginner
Channel Scrambler	Theta Music	Online	Timbre Recognition	Responding	Advanced
Compose It	New Bedford Symphony Orchestra	Online	Composition	Creating	Advanced
Compose with Us Now	Inside the Orchestra	Online	Melodic Composition	Creating	Intermediate
Compose Your Own Music	Classics for Kids	Online	Composition	Creating	Intermediate
Cyber Pattern Player	PBS Kids	Online	Melodic Composition	Creating	Beginner
Daniel Tiger: Feel the Music	PBS Kids	Online	Melody Exploration	Connecting	Beginner
Flashnote Derby	Luke Bartolomeo	iPad	Notation Training	Responding	Intermediate
Incredibox	So Far So Good	iPad, Online	Composition	Creating	Intermediate
Instrument Match	Music Teacher's Games	Online	Instrument Timbre	Responding	Intermediate
Isle of Tune	Happylander Ltd.	iPad, Online	Composition	Connecting	Intermediate
Kandinsky	Chrome Music Lab	Online	Composition	Connecting	Beginner
Match the Rhythm	Classics for Kids	Online	Rhythmic Performance	Responding	Beginner
Mario Paint Music Composer	unFun Games	Online	Composition	Creating	Advanced
Melody Maker	Chrome Music Lab	Online	Composition	Responding	Beginner
Minecraft Open Note Block Studio	Open NBS	Online	Composition	Creating	Advanced
Music Maps	Inside the Orchestra	Online	Music Mapping	Connecting	Intermediate

Game Title	Developer	OS	Concept	Standard	Level
Musical Me!	Duck Duck Moose	iOS	Various	Responding	Beginner
Note Fighter	Mythic Owl	iOS	Piano Practice	Performing	Advanced
Note Names	Classics for Kids	Online	Notation Training	Responding	Intermediate
Online Rhythm Composer	Inside the Orchestra	Online	Rhythmic Composition	Creating	Intermediate
Otogarden	Constantino Oliva	Online	Melodic Composition	Creating	Intermediate
Paint with Music	Google Arts and Culture	Online	Melodic Composition	Connecting	Beginner
Parrot Phrases	Theta Music	Online	Aural Perception	Responding	Advanced
Peg + Cat Music Maker	PBS Kids	Online	Performing Music	Performing	Beginner
Perfect Pitch	The Kennedy Center	Online	Instrument Quiz	Connecting	Advanced
Piano Dust Buster	JoyTunes	iOS	Piano Practice	Performing	Intermediate
Pinkamusical Garden	PBS Kids	Online	Composition	Responding	Beginner
Pitchy Ninja	Pitchy Ninja	Online	Vocal Training	Performing	Advanced
Rhythm Cat	Melody Cats	iOS	Rhythmic Practice	Performing	Intermediate
Rhythm Maker	Chrome Music Lab	Online	Composition	Creating	Beginner
Slap Track	Honey Doo Dat	Online	Rhythmic Practice	Performing	Beginner
Sorglio	Encore	Online	Song Identification	Connecting	Advanced
Song Maker	Chrome Music Lab	Online	Composition	Creating	Beginner
Spectrogram	Google	Online	Exploration	Connecting	Beginner
Staff Dungeon	Doctor Musik	Online	Notation Training	Responding	Intermediate
Staff Wars	TMI Media	iOS	Notation Training	Responding	Intermediate
Tonic Finder	Theta Music	Online	Aural Perception	Responding	Advanced
Vocal Match	Theta Music	Online	Vocal Training	Performing	Advanced
Young Person's Guide to the Orchestra	Carnegie Hall Listening Adventures	Online	Orchestra Identification	Connecting	Intermediate

References

Abrahams, D. (2018). Engaging music students through Minecraft. *Proceedings of the ICERI2018 Conference*. Seville, Spain: International Education Conference.

Abt, C. (1970). *Serious games*. New York, NY: Viking Press.

Age of Learning. (2019). *Adventure Academy* [Computer software]. Glendale, CA: Age of Learning.

Ahmad, M. (2020). Categorizing game design elements into educational game design fundamentals. In I. Deliyannis. (Ed.), *Game design and intelligent interaction*. Intechopen. Retrieved from https://www.intechopen.com/chapters/70106

Anderson, C. A., & Bushman, B. J. (2001). Effects of violent video games on aggressive behavior, aggressive cognition, aggressive affect, physiological arousal, and prosocial behavior: A meta-analytic review of the scientific literature. *Psychological Science*, *12*(5), 353–359.

Anderson, C., & Dill, K. (2000). Video games and aggressive thoughts, feelings, and behavior in the laboratory and in life. *Journal of Personality and Social Psychology*, *78*(4), 772–790. doi:10.1037/0022-3514.78.4.772

Anderson, W. (2011). The Dalcroze approach to music education: Theory and applications. *General Music Today*, *26*(1), 27–33.

Annetta, L. (2008). Video games in education: Why they should be used and how they are being used. *Theory into Practice*, *47*, 229–239.

Annetta, L. (2010). The "I's" have it: A framework for serious educational game design. *Review of General Psychology*, *14*(2), 105–112. doi:10.1037/a0018985

Annetta, L., Murray, M., Laird, S., Bohr, S., & Park, J. (2006). Serious games: Incorporating video games into the classroom. *Educause Quarterly*, *1*(3), 16–22.

Archbell, C. L. (2009). *Covert learning: Perceptions of video games and education* (Order No. MR53258). Available from ProQuest Dissertations & Theses Global. (305068722). Retrieved from http://ezproxy.cul.columbia.edu/login?url=http://search.proquest.com/docview/30506872   2?accountid=10226

Arrasvuori, J. (2006). *Playing and making music: Exploring the similarities between video games and music-making software*. Doctoral dissertation, University of Tempere, Tampere, Finland. Retrieved from https://tampub.uta.fi/bitstream/handle/10024/67626/951-44-6689-6.pdf?sequence=1

Arrasvuori, J., & Holm, J. (2010, October). *Background music reactive games*. Paper presented at *MindTrek 2010*, Tampere, Finland.

Arsenault, D. (2008). Guitar Hero: "Not like playing guitar at all"? *Loading. . . .*, *2*(2), 1–7. Retrieved from http://journals.sfu.ca/loading/index.php/loading/article/viewArticle/32

Auerbach, B. (2010). Pedagogical applications of the video game Dance Dance Revolution to aural skills instruction. *Society for Music Theory*, *16*(1), 1–38.

Austin, M. (Ed.). (2016). *Music video games: Performance, politics, and play*. New York, NY: Bloomsbury.

Backlund, P., & Hendrix, M. (2013, September). Educational games: Are they worth the effort? A literature survey of the effectiveness of serious games. In *Games and virtual worlds for serious applications (VS-GAMES), 2013 5th International Conference on Games and Virtual Worlds for Serious Applications* (pp. 1–8.). Institute of Electrical and Electronics Engineers.

Baek, Y. (2008). What hinders teachers in using computer and video games in the classroom? Exploring factors inhibiting the uptake of computer and video games. *CyberPsychology & Behavior*, *11*(6), 665–671.

Barab, S., Gresalfi, M., & Arici, A. (2009). Why educators should care about games. *Educational Leadership*, *67*(1), 76–80.

Bartolomeo, L. (2014). *Flashnote Derby* [Computer software]. Chicago, IL: Luke Bartolomeo.

Beat Games. (2019). *Beat Saber* [Computer software]. Prague, Czech Republic: Beat Games.

Benedict, C. (2010). Curriculum. In H. Abeles & L. Custodero (Eds.), *Critical issues in music education: Contemporary theory and practice* (pp. 143–166). New York, NY: Oxford University Press.

References

Benedict, C., & O'Leary, J. (2019). Reconceptualizing "music making:" Music technology and freedom in the age of neoliberalism. *Action, Criticism, and Theory for Music Education, 18*(1), 26–43.

Bensiger, J. (2012). *Perceptions of pre-service teachers of using video games as teaching tools* (Order No 3517303). Available from ProQuest Dissertations & Theses Global. (1032539592). Retrieved from http://ezproxy.cul.columbia.edu/login?url=http://search.proquest.com/docview/1032539592?accountid=10226

Bian, H. (2016). Application of virtual reality in music teaching system. *iJET, 11*(11), 21–25.

Blizzard Entertainment. (2004). *World of Warcraft* [Computer software]. Irvine, CA: Blizzard Entertainment.

Böshe, W., & Kattner, F. (2011). Fear of (serious) digital games and game-based learning? Causes, consequences, and a possible countermeasure. *International Journal of Game-Based Learning, 1*(3), 1–15.

Brøderbund Software. (1985). *Where in the world Is Carmen Sandiego?* [Computer software]. Eugene, OR: Brøderbund.

Brown, K. (2014). *Prelude—An augmented reality iOS application for music education.* Honors Projects, Bowling Green University, 112.

Burns, A. (2020). *Using technology with elementary music approaches.* New York, NY: Oxford University Press.

Campo Santo. (2016). *Firewatch* [Computer software]. San Francisco, CA: Campo Santo.

Carnegie Hall. (2021). *Young Person's Guide to the Orchestra* [Computer software]. Retrieved from https://listeningadventures.carnegiehall.org/?ReturnUrl=%2Ftuba_game

Castronova, E. (2007). *Exodus to the virtual world.* New York, NY: Palgrave Macmillan.

Chen, W. (2022). Research on the design of intelligent music teaching system based on virtual reality technology. *Hindawi, 2022,* Article ID: 7832306.

Cheng, W. (2014). *Sound play: Video games and the musical imagination.* New York, NY: Oxford University Press.

Cheppudira, M. (2020). *Pitchy Ninja* [Computer software]. Retrieved from https://pitchy.ninja

Childress, M., & Braswell, R. (2006). Using massively multiplayer online role-playing games for online learning. *Distance Education, 27*(2), 187–196.

The Chinese Room. (2012). *Dear Esther* [Computer software]. Brighton, UK: The Chinese Room.

Cincinnati Public Radio. (2022). *Compose Your Own Music* [Computer software]. Retrieved from https://www.classicsforkids.com/music-games

Classics for Kids. (2022). *Match the Rhythm* [Computer software]. Retrieved from https://www.classicsforkids.com/music-games

Classics for Kids. (2023). *Note Names* [Computer software]. Retrieved from https://www.classicsforkids.com/music-games

Clement, K. (2021). Using augmented reality in classical music. *Arts Management and Technology Laboratory.* Retrieved from https://amt-lab.org/blog/2021/8/using-augmented-reality-in-classical-music

The College Board. (2013). *International Standards for Arts Education: A review of standards, practices, and expectations in thirteen countries and regions.* New York, NY: National Coalition for Core Arts Standards.

Cook, M. (2019). Augmented reality: Examining its value in a music technology classroom. Practice and potential. *Waikato Journal of Education, 24*(2), 23–38.

Criswell, C. (2009). Music technology: Can video games be educational? *Teaching Music, 16*(6), 24–26.

Csikszentmihalyi, M. (1975a). *Beyond boredom and anxiety: Experiencing flow in work and play.* San Francisco, CA: Jossey-Bass.

Csikszentmihalyi, M. (1975b). Play and intrinsic rewards. *Journal of Humanistic Psychology, 15*(3), 41–63.

Csikszentmihalyi, M. (1990). *Flow: The psychology of optimal experience.* New York, NY: Harper Collins.

Dalcroze Society of America. (2022). What is Dalcroze? *Dalcroze USA.* Retrieved from https://dalcrozeusa.org/about-dalcroze/what-is-dalcroze

Dammers, R., & LoPresti, M. (2020). *Practical music education technology*. New York, NY: Oxford University Press.

Davidson & Associates. (1983). *Math Blaster!* [Computer software]. Torrance, CA: Davidson.

deHaan, J., Reed, W., & Kuwada, K. (2010). The effect of interactivity with a music video game on second language vocabulary recall. *Language Learning and Technology, 14*(2), 74–94.

Denis, G., & Jouvelot, P. (2005, June). Motivation-driven educational game design: Applying best practices to music education. In *Proceedings of the 2005 ACM SIGCHI International Conference on Advances in Computer Entertainment Technology* (pp. 462–465). ACM. doi:10.1145/1178477.1178581

Deterding, S., Dixon, D., Khaled, R., & Nacke, L. (2011, September). From game design elements to gamefulness: defining gamification. In *Proceedings of the 15th International Academic MindTrek Conference: Envisioning future media environments* (pp. 9–15). Association for Computer Machinery.

devCAT. (2008). *Mabinogi* [Computer software]. Tokyo, Japan: Nexon Co., Ltd.

Dewey, J. (1938). *Experience and education*. New York, NY: Free Press.

Diaz, C., Hincapié, M., & Moreno, G. (2015). How the type of content in educative augmented reality application affects the learning experience. *Procedia Computer Science, 75*, 205–212.

Dicheva, D., Dichev, C., Agre, G., & Angelova, G. (2015). Gamification in education: A systematic mapping study. *International Forum of Educational Technology & Society, 18*(3), 75–88. Retrieved from http://www.jstor.org/stable/jeductechsoci.18.3.75

Dillon, T. (2003). Collaborating and creating on music technologies. *International Journal of Educational Research, 39*(1), 893–897.

Dondlinger, M. (2007). Educational video game design: A review of the literature. *Journal of Applied Educational Technology, 4*(1), 21–31.

Donovan, T. (2010). *Replay: The history of video games*. East Sussex: Yellow Ant.

Drool. (2016). *Thumper* [Computer software]. Bristol, UK: Drool.

Duck Duck Moose. (2021). *Musical Me!* [Computer software]. Garden City, NY: Duck Duck Moose.

Egenfeldt-Nielsen, S., Smith, J., & Tosca, S. (2016). *Understanding video games: The essential introduction*. New York, NY: Routledge.

Encore. (2014). *Songlio* [Computer software]. Retrieved from https://songl.io

Entertainment Software Association (ESA). (2023). Essential facts about the computer and video game industry. Retrieved from https://www.theesa.com/2023-essential-facts

Gee, E., & Tran, K. (2016). Video game making and modding. In B. Guzzetti & M. Lesley. (Eds.), *Handbook of research on the societal impact of social media* (pp. 238–267). Hershey, PA: IGI Global.

Gee, J. (2005). Learning by design: Good video games as learning machines. *E-Learning, 2*(1), 5–16.

Gee, J. (2013). *Good video games + good learning: Collected essays on video games, learning, and literacy*. New York, NY: Peter Lang.

Gee, J. P. (2003). *What video games have to teach us about learning and literacy*. New York, NY: Palgrave Macmillan.

Gee, J. P. (2007). *What video games have to teach us about learning and literacy*. 2nd ed. New York, NY: Palgrave Macmillan.

Giant Sparrow. (2017). *What remains of Edith Finch* [Computer software]. West Hollywood, CA: Annapurna Interactive.

Google. (2016). *Chrome Music Lab: Kandinsky* [Computer software]. Retrieved from https://musiclab.chromeexperiments.com/Kandinsky

Google. (2016). *Chrome Music Lab: Rhythm Maker* [Computer software]. Retrieved from https://musiclab.chromeexperiments.com/rhythm

Google. (2016). *Chrome Music Lab: Song Maker* [Computer software]. Retrieved from https://musiclab.chromeexperiments.com/Song-Maker

Google. (2016). *Chrome Music Lab: Spectrogram* [Computer software]. Retrieved from https://musiclab.chromeexperiments.com/Spectrogram

Google. (2016). *Melody Maker* [Computer software]. Retrieved from https://musiclab.chromeexperiments.com/Melody-Maker

References

Gower, L., & McDowell, J. (2012). Interactive music video games and children's musical development. *British Journal of Music Education, 29*(1), 91–105. doi:10.1017/SO265051711000398

Granic, I., Lobel, A., & Engles, R. (2014). The benefits of playing video games. *American Psychologist, 69*(1), 66–78. doi:10.1037/a0034857

Grimm, L. (1986). *Reader Rabbit* [Computer software]. Boston: The Learning Company.

Grooten, J., & Kowert, R. (2015). Going beyond the game: Development of gamer identities within societal discourse and virtual spaces. *The Journal of the Canadian Game Studies Association, 9*(14), 70–87.

Gulu, H., Kocer, S., & Dundar, O. (2021). Application of augmented reality in music education. *The Eurasia Proceedings of Science, Technology, Engineering, and Mathematics, 14*, 45–56.

Hämäläinen, P., Mäki-Patola, T., Pulkki, V., & Airas, M. (2004, October). Musical computer games played by singing. In *Proceedings of the 7th International Conference. on Digital Audio Effects (DAFx'04), Naples*.

Han, S. (2021). The implications of combining augmented reality and virtual reality with music. *Fordham University*. Retrieved from http://www.fordhamiplj.org/2021/11/11/the- implications-of-combining-augmented-reality-and-virtual-reality-with-music

HappyLander, Inc. (2014). *Isle of Tune* [Computer software]. Retrieved from https://isleoftune.com

Harmonix. (2001). *Karaoke Revolution* [Computer software]. Boston: Harmonix.

Harmonix. (2005). *Guitar Hero* [Computer software]. Cambridge, MA: Harmonix.

Harmonix. (2008). *Rock Band* [Computer software]. Cambridge, MA: Harmonix.

Harmonix. (2014). *Fantasia: Music Evolved* [XBox 360]. Glendale, CA: Disney Interactive.

Hein, E. (2014). Music games in education. In A. Ruthmann & R. Mantie. (Eds.), *The Oxford handbook of technology and music education*. New York, NY: Oxford University Press, 93–108.

Human Entertainment. (1989). *Dance Aerobics* [Nintendo Entertainment System]. Kyoto, Japan: Nintendo.

Ibrahim, A., Vela, F., Rodríguiez, P., Sánchez, J., & Zea, N. (2012). Playability guidelines for educational video games: A comprehensive and integrated literature review. *International Journal of Game-Based Learning, 2*(4), 18–40. doi:10.4018/ijgbl.2012100102

Inside the Orchestra. (2020). *Compose Your Own Song* [Computer software]. Retrieved from https://insidetheorchestra.org/2020/03/25/composing-for-kids

Inside the Orchestra. (2020). *Online Rhythm Composer* [Computer software]. Retrieved from https://insidetheorchestra.org/2020/03/25/composing-for-kids

Inside the Orchestra. (2022). *Music Maps* [Computer software]. Retrieved from https://insidetheorchestra.org/musical-games

International Society for Technology in Education. (2022). ISTE standards for students. *ISTE*. Retrieved from https://www.iste.org/standards/iste-standards-for-students

Jam Studio VR. (2020). *Jam Studio VR* [Computer software]. Scottsdale, AZ: Beamz Interactive.

Jenson, J., De Castell, S., Muehrer, R., & Droumeva, M. (2016). So you think you can play: An exploratory study of music video games. *Journal of Music, Technology, and Education, 9*(3), 273–288.

JoyTunes. (2013). *Piano Dust Buster* [Computer software]. Retrieved from https://apps.apple.com/us/app/piano-dust-buster-by-joytunes/id502356539

Kapp, K. (2012). *The gamification of learning and instruction: Game-based methods and strategies for training and education*. Hoboken, NJ: John Wiley & Sons.

Kayali, F., & Pichlmair, M. (2008). Playing music and playing games: Simulation vs. gameplay in music-based games. In *FROG-Vienna Games Conference* (p. 12). Phaidra, Universität Wien.

Keeler, K. (2020). Video games in music education: The impact of video games on rhythmic performance. *Visions of Research in Music Education, 37*. Retrieved from http://www.rider.edu/~vrme

The Kennedy Center. (2007). *Perfect Pitch* [Computer software]. Retrieved from https://artsedge.kennedy-center.org/interactives/perfectpitch2/index.html

Kersten, F. (2006). Inclusion of technology resources in early childhood music education. *General Music Today, 20*(1), 15–28.

Koehler, M. (2012). TPACK explained. *TPACK.org*. Retrieved from http://www.tpack.org

Kolb, L. (2020). About the Triple E Framework. *Triple E Framework*. Retrieved from https://www.tripleeframework.com/about.html

Konami. (1998). *Dance Dance Revolution* [Computer software]. Tokyo, Japan: Konami.
Koster, R. (2014). *A theory of fun for game design*. Sabastopol, CA: O'Reilly.
Kuhn, W., & Allvin, R. (1967). Computer-assisted teaching: A new approach to research in music. *Journal of Research in Music Education 15*(4), 305–315.
Kutner, L., & Olson, C. (2008). *Grand theft childhood: The surprising truth about violent video games*. New York, NY: Simon & Schuster.
Lazzaro, N. (2004). Why we play games: Four keys to more emotion without story [Abstract]. In *Player experience: Research and design for mass market interactive entertainment* (pp. 1–8). Oakland, CA: XEODesign.
The Learning Company. (1983). *Reader Rabbit* [Computer software]. Palo Alto, CA: The Learning Company.
Lesser, A. (2020). An investigation of digital game-based learning software in the elementary general music classroom. *Journal of Sound of Music in Games, 1*(2), 1–24.
Linden Lab. (2003). *Second Life* [Computer software]. San Francisco, CA: Linden Research.
Loftus, G., & Loftus, E. (1983). *Mind at play: The psychology of video games*. New York, NY: Basic Books.
London Studio. (2004). *SingStar* [Computer software]. London: Sony.
Lu, Y., Wang, X., Gong, J., & Liang, Y. (2022). ChordAR: An educational AR game design for children's music theory learning. *Wireless Communications and Mobile Computing*, 1–9.
Major, C. (2015). *Teaching online: A guide to teaching, research, and practice*. Baltimore, MD: Johns Hopkins University Press.
Márquez, I. (2014). Playing new music with old games: The chiptune subculture. *G|A|M|E| Games as Art, Media, Entertainment, 1*(3), 67–79.
Mattoo, S. (2022). What is virtual reality? The bright future of immersive technology. *G2*. Retrieved from https://www.g2.com/articles/virtual-reality
Maxis. (2002). *The Sims Online* [Computer software]. Redwood City, CA: EA Games.
McDermott, J. (Ed.). (1981). *The Philosophy of John Dewey*. Chicago. IL: University of Chicago Press.
McGonigal, J. (2011). *Reality is broken: Why games make us better and how they can change the world*. New York: Penguin Press.
MECC. (1974). *The Oregon Trail* [Computer software]. Brooklyn Center, MO: Minnesota Educational Computing Consortium.
Media Molecule. (2008). *Little Big Planet* [Computer software]. Tokyo, Japan: Sony Interactive Entertainment.
Meier, S. (1991). *Civilization* [Computer software]. Hunt Valley, MD: MicroProse.
Melnick, K. (2022). This AR drum app could revolutionize music learning. *VR Scout*. Retrieved from https://vrscout.com/news/this-ar-drum-app-could-revolutionize-music-learning
Melody Cats. (2017). *Rhythm Cat* [Computer software]. Retrieved from https://melodycats.com/rhythm-cat
Messina, E. (2021). School of music professors unite conducting and virtual reality with *RibbonsVR*. Illinois State University. Retrieved from https://news.illinoisstate.edu/2021/11/school-of-music-professors-unite-conducting-and- virtual-reality-with-ribbonsvr
Miller, B. (2013). Music learning through video games and apps. *American Music, 31*(4), 511+.
Miller, K. (2009). Schizophonic performance: *Guitar Hero, Rock Band*, and virtual virtuosity. *Journal for the Society of American Music, 3*(4), 395–429. doi:10.1017/S1752196309990666
Miller, K. (2012). *Playing along: Digital games, YouTube, and virtual performance*. New York, NY: Oxford University Press.
Mishra, P., & Koehler, M. (2006). Technological pedagogical content knowledge: A framework for teacher knowledge. *Teachers College Record, 108*(6), 1017–1054.
Missingham, A. (2007). *Why console-games are bigger than rock n' roll* [Unpublished manuscript].
Mojang. (2011). *Minecraft* [Computer software]. Stockholm, Sweden: Mojang.
Murillo, R. (2017). The 21st century elementary music classroom and the digital music curriculum: A synergism of technology and traditional pedagogy. *Texas Music Education Research, 14*(1), 14–27.
Myllykoski, M., Tuuri, K., Viirret, E., & Louhivuori, J. (2015). Prototyping hand-based wearable music education technology. *Proceedings of the International Conference on New Interfaces for Music Expression*, Baton Rouge, LA.

MythicOwl. (2020). *Note Fighter* [Computer software]. Retrieved from https://play.google.com/store/apps/details?id=net.notefighter.android&hl=en_US&gl=US

Namco. (2004). *Taiko Drum Master* [PlayStation 2]. Tokyo, Japan: Namco.

Nesky, J. (2011). *Beepbox* [Computer software]. Retrieved from https://www.beepbox.co

New Bedford Symphony Orchestra. (2022). *Compose It* [Computer software]. Retrieved from https://nbsymphony.org/compose-it

Niantic. (2016). *Pokémon Go* [Computer software]. San Francisco, CA: Niantic.

Nijs, L. (2018). Dalcroze meets technology: Integrating music, movement, and visuals with the Music Paint Machine. *Music Education Research, 20*(2), 163–183.

Nintendo. (1985). *Super Mario Bros.* [Nintendo Entertainment System]. Kyoto, Japan: Nintendo.

Nintendo. (1986). *The Legend of Zelda* [Nintendo Entertainment System]. Kyoto, Japan: Nintendo.

Nintendo. (1992). *Mario Paint* [Computer software]. Kyoto, Japan: Nintendo.

Nintendo. (2004). *Donkey Konga* [Nintendo GameCube]. Kyoto, Japan: Nintendo.

Nintendo. (2008). *Wii Music* [Nintendo Wii]. Kyoto, Japan: Nintendo.

Nintendo. (2015). *Super Mario Maker* [Computer software]. Kyoto, Japan: Nintendo.

Nintendo. (2020). *Animal Crossing: New Horizons* [Nintendo Switch]. Kyoto, Japan: Nintendo.

O'Leary, J. (2020). Applications of affinity space characteristics in music education. In J. Waldron, S. Horsley, & K. Veblen, *The Oxford Handbook of social media and music learning* (pp. 65–88). New York, NY: Oxford University Press.

O'Leary, J., & Tobias, E. (2016). Sonic participatory cultures within, through, and around video games. In R. Mantie & G. Smith. (Eds.), *The Oxford Handbook of Music Making and Leisure* (pp. 543–566). Oxford: Oxford University Press.

O'Meara, D. (2016). *Rocksmith* and the shaping of player experience. In M. Austin. (Ed.), *Music video games: Performance, politics, and play*. New York, NY: Bloomsbury.

Oliva, C. (2021). *Otogarden* [Computer software]. Retrieved from https://otogarden.com

Oliva, C. (2022). *Otogarden*: Exploring musical improvisation in video games. *Journal of Sound and Music in Games, 3*(2), 2578–3432.

Open NBS. (2002). *Minecraft Open Note Block Studio* [Computer software]. Retrieved from https://opennbs.org

Origin Systems. (1997). *Ultima Online* [Computer software]. Redwood City, CA: EA Games.

Paney, A., & Kay, A. (2014). Developing singing in third-grade music classrooms: The effect of a concurrent-feedback computer game on pitch-matching skills. *Update: Applications of Research in Music Education, 34*(1), 1–8.

Pangsakulyanont, T., & Suktarachan, N. (2022). *Bemuse: Beat Music Sequencer* [Computer software]. Retrieved from https://bemuse.ninja

Parkin, S. (2022). The trouble with Roblox, the video game empire built on child labour. *The Guardian.* Retrieved from https://www.theguardian.com/games/2022/jan/09/the-trouble-with-roblox-the-video-game-empire-built-on-child-labour

Patterson, G. (2020). The Kodály approach to teaching music. In A. Burns (Ed.), *Using technology with elementary school approaches* (pp. 75–84). New York, NY: Oxford University Press.

Pavlenko, O., Shcherbak, I., Hura, V., Lihus, V., Maidaniuk, I., & Skoryk, T. (2022). Development of music education in virtual and extended reality. *Brain: Broad Research in Artificial Intlligence and Neuroscience, 13*, no. (3), 308–319.

PBS Kids. (1999). *Carmen's World Orchestra* [Computer software]. Retrieved from https://pbskids.org/luna/games/carmens-world-orchestra

PBS Kids. (1999). *Peg + Cat Music Maker* [Computer software]. Retrieved from https://pbskids.org/peg/games/music-maker

PBS Kids. (2018). *Cyber Pattern Player* [Computer software]. Retrieved from https://pbskids.org/cyberchase/games/cyber-pattern-player

PBS Kids. (2020). *Daniel Tiger: Feel the Music* [Computer software]. Retrieved from https://pbskids.org/daniel/games/feel-the-music

PBS Kids. (2023). *Pinkamusical Garden* [Computer software]. Retrieved from https://pbskids.org/pinkalicious/games/pinkamusical-garden

Peppler, K., Downton, M., Lindsay, E., & Hay, K. (2011). The Nirvana effect: Tapping video games to mediate music learning and interest. *International Journal of Learning and Media*, 3(1), 41–59.

Piaget, J. (1962). *Play, dreams and imitation in childhood*. New York, NY: Norton.

Pichlmair, M., & Kayali, F. (2007, September). Levels of sound: On the principles of interactivity in music video games. In *Proceedings of the Digital Games Research Association 2007 Conference on Situated Play*.

Pink, D. (2009). *Drive: The surprising truth about what motivates us*. New York, NY: Riverhead.

Prensky, M. (2001). *Digital game-based learning*. New York, NY: McGraw-Hill.

Prensky, M. (2006). *Don't bother me Mom—I'm learning!* St. Paul: Paragon House.

Prodigy Education, Inc. (2011). *Prodigy* [Computer software]. Oakville, CA: Prodigy Education, Inc.

Puentedura, R. (2021, November 4–5). *Using games in education: A pragmatic approach* [Conference presentation]. Vermont Fest 2021, Killington, VT, United States. http://hippasus.com/rrpweblog/archives/2021/11/UsingGamesInEducation_PragmaticAp proach.pdf

Rare. (2018). *Sea of Thieves* [Computer software]. Redmond, WA: Microsoft Studios.

Rawitsch, D., Heinemann, B., & Dillenberger, P. (1971). *The Oregon Trail* [Computer software]. Brooklyn Center, MN: MECC.

Reality Reflection, Inc. (2016). *Music Inside* [Computer software]. Seoul, Korea: Reality Reflection Inc.

Really Interactive. (2020). *Virtuoso VR* [Computer software]. Stockholm, Sweden: Really Interactive.

Richardson, P., & Kim, Y. (2011). Beyond fun and games: A framework for quantifying music skill developments from video game play. *Journal of New Music Research*, 40(4), 277–291. doi:10.1080/09299215.2011.565350

Rigby, S., & Ryan, R. (2011). *Glued to games: How video games draw us in and hold us spellbound*. Westport, CT: Praeger.

Roesner, D., Paisley, A., & Cassidy, G. (2016). Guitar heroes in the classroom: The creative potential of music games. In M. Austin. (Ed.), *Music video games: Performance, politics, and play*. New York, NY: Bloomsbury.

Rooney, P. (2012). A theoretical framework for serious game design: Exploring pedagogy, play, and fidelity and their implications for the design process. *International Journal of Game- Based Learning*, 2(4), 41–60.

Roulston, K. (2002). Revisiting Kodály's writings on early childhood music education: Implications for teaching in the 21st century. *Bulletin (Kodaly Music Education Institute of Australia)*, (2002–2003), 26–39.

Rucsanda, M., Belibou, A., & Cazan, A. (2021). Students' attitudes toward online music education during the COVID-19 lockdown. *Frontiers in Psychology*, 12(753785), 1–10.

Ryan, R., Rigby, C., & Przybylski, A. (2006). The motivational pull of video games: A self- determination approach. *Motivation and Emotion*, 30(4), 344–361. doi:10.1007/s11031- 006-9051-8

Sáez-López, J., Miller, J., Vásquez-Cano, E., & Garrido, D. (2015). Exploring application, attitudes, and integration of video games: *MinecraftEdu* in middle school. *Journal of Educational Technology & Society*, 18(3), 114–128. Retrieved from http://www.jstor.org/stable/jeductechsoci.18.3.114

Salen, K., & Zimmerman, E. (2004). *Rules of play: Game design fundamentals*. Cambridge, MA: MIT Press.

Shaffer, D. (2006). *How computer games help children learn*. New York, NY: Palgrave Macmillan.

Sheldon, L. (2012). *The multiplayer classroom: Designing coursework as a game*. Boston: Cengage.

Shute, V. (2011). Stealth assessment in computer-based games to support learning. In S. Tobias & J. Fletcher (Eds.). *Computer games and instruction* (pp. 503–524). Charlotte, NC: Information Age Publishing.

Singularity 6. (2023). *Palia* [Computer software]. Los Angeles, CA: Singularity 6, Inc.

Smith, J. (2004). I can see tomorrow in your dance: A study of Dance Dance Revolution and music video games. *Journal of Popular Music Studies*, 16(1), 58–84. doi:10.1111/j.0022-4146.2004.00011x

Smuts, A. (2009). What is interactivity? *Journal of Aesthetic Education*, 43(4), 53–73. Retrieved from http://www.jstor.org/stable/25656247

So Far So Good. (2009). *Incredibox* [Computer software]. Retrieved from https://www.incredibox.com

Sonic Team. (1999). *Samba de Amigo* [Computer software]. Tokyo, Japan: Sega.

178 References

Sony Computer Entertainment. (2014). *Little Big Planet 3* [Computer software]. Sheffield, UK: Sumo Digital Ltd.

Square Enix. (2013). *Final Fantasy XIV* [Computer software]. Tokyo, Japan: Square Enix.

Squire, K. (2011). *Video games and learning: Teaching and participatory culture in the digital age.* New York, NY: Teachers College Press.

Standing Stone Games. (2007). *The Lord of the Rings Online* [Computer software]. San Diego, CA: Daybreak Game Company LLC.

Strong, M. (2020). The Feieraband approach. In A. Burns (Ed.), *Using technology with elementary school approaches* (pp. 19–25). New York, NY: Oxford University Press.

Symphonic Games. (2023). *Maestro VR* [Computer software]. Barcelona, Spain: Symphonic Games.

TCW. (2019). *Spatial Orchestra* [Computer software]. Los Angeles, CA: TCW.

TeacherGaming. (2011). *MinecraftEDU* [Computer software]. Stockholm, Sweden: Mojang.

Terada, Y. (2020). A powerful model for understanding good tech integration. *Edutopia*. Retrieved from https://www.edutopia.org/article/powerful-model-understanding-good- tech-integration

Theta Music Trainer. (2014). *Vocal Match* [Computer software]. Retrieved from https://trainer.thetamusic.com/en/content/html5-vocal-match

Theta Music Trainer. (2023). *Band Match* [Computer software]. Retrieved from https://trainer.thetamusic.com/en/content/html5-band-match

Theta Music Trainer. (2023). *Channel Scramble* [Computer software]. Retrieved from https://trainer.thetamusic.com/en/content/html5-channel-match

Theta Music Trainer. (2023). *Instrument Match* [Computer software]. Retrieved from http://musicteachersgames.com/instrument1

Theta Music Trainer. (2023). *Parrot Phrases* [Computer software]. Retrieved from https://trainer.thetamusic.com/en/content/html5-parrot-phrases

Theta Music Trainer. (2023). *Tonic Finder* [Computer software]. Retrieved from https://trainer.thetamusic.com/en/content/html5-tonic-finder

TMI Media, LLC. (2014). *Staff Wars* [Computer software]. Norwalk, CT: TMI Media.

Tobias, E. (2012). Let's play! Learning music through video games and virtual worlds. In G. McPherson & G. Welch. (Eds.), *The Oxford Handbook of Music Education, Vol. 2* (pp. 531–548). New York, NY: Oxford University Press.

Tobias, E. (2020). Envisioning pedagogical possibilities of social media and sonic participatory cultures. In J. Waldron, S. Horsley, & K. Veblen, *The Oxford Handbook of Social Media and Music Learning* (pp. 40–63). New York, NY: Oxford University Press.

Tobias, E., & O'Leary, J. (2016). Video games. In A. King, E. Himonides, & S. Ruthmann. (Eds.), *The Routledge Companion to Music, Technology, and Education* (pp. 263–272). New York, NY: Routledge.

Turbine. (2007). *The Lord of the Rings Online* [Computer software]. Needham, MA: Turbine.

Ubisoft. (2009). *Just Dance* [Computer software]. Rennes, France: Ubisoft.

Ubisoft. (2011). *Rocksmith* [Computer software]. San Francisco, CA: Ubisoft.

Ubisoft. (2014). *Just Dance Now* [Computer software]. Rennes, France: Ubisoft.

unfun Games. (2008). *Mario Paint Composer* [Computer software]. Retrieved from https://minghai.github.io/MarioSequencer

United Game Artists. (2015). *Rez Infinite* [Computer software]. Tokyo, Japan: Sega.

Van Eck, R. (2006). Digital game based learning: It's not just the digital natives who are restless. *EDUCAUSE Review, 41*(2), 16. Retrieved from https://www.researchgate.net/publication/242513283

Verant Interactive. (1999). *EverQuest* [Computer software]. San Diego, CA: Sony Online Entertainment.

Vygotsky, L. (1978). *Mind in society: The development of higher psychological processes.* Cambridge, MA: Harvard University Press.

Waddington, D. (2015). Dewey and video games: From education through occupations to education through simulations. *Educational Theory, 65*(1), 1–20.

Webster, P. (2002). Historical perspectives on technology and music. *Music Educators Journal,* 8

Wechselberger, U. (2016). Music game enjoyment and natural mapping beyond intuitiveness. *Simulation & Gaming, 47*(3), 304–323. doi:10.1177/1046878116651024

World Health Organization. (2020). Addictive behaviours: Gaming disorder. *World Health Organization*. Retrieved from https://www.who.int/news-room/questions-and-answers/item/addictive-behaviours-gaming-disorder

Xiao, H. (2022). Innovation of digital multimedia VR technology in music education curriculum in colleges and universities. *Scientific Programming, 2022*(1), 6566144.

XL Games. (2014). *ArcheAge* [Computer software]. Seoul, Korea: XL Games.

Young, M., Slota, S., Cutter, A., Jalette, G., Mullin, G., Lai, B. . . . Yukhymenko, M. (2012). Our princess is in another castle: A review of trends in serious gaming for education. *Review of Educational Research, 82*(1), 61–89. doi:10.3102/0034654312436980

Index of List of Games Cited

For the benefit of digital users, indexed terms that span two pages (e.g., 52-53) may, on occasion, appear on only one of those pages.

Band Match, 107–9
Beast Box, 132–33
BeepBox, 138–41
BeMuse: Beat Music Sequencer, 76–78

Carmen's World Orchestra, 63–64
Channel Scrambler, 104–7
Chrome Music Lab: Kandinsky, 118–20
Compose It, 53–55
Compose With Us Now, 49–50
Compose Your Own Music, 46–48
Cyber Pattern Player, 36–40

Daniel Tiger: Feel The Music, 116–17

Flashnote Derby, 95–97

Incredibox, 51–53
Instrument Match, 102–4
Isle of Tune, 129–31

Mario Paint Composer, 55–58
Match the Rhythm, 69–71
Melody Maker, 89–91
Minecraft Open Note Block Studio, 58–60
Musical Me!, 91–93
Music Maps, 127–29

Note Fighter, 78–80
Note Names, 93–95

Online Rhythm Composer, 42–44
Otogarden, 44–46

Paint With Music, 122–24
Parrot Phrases, 112–14
Peg + Cat Music Maker, 65–67
Perfect Pitch, 134–36
Piano Dust Buster & Piano Dust Buster 2, 74–76
Pinkamusical Garden, 87–88
Pitchy Ninja, 82–84

Slap Track, 67–69
Song Maker, 40–42
Songlio, 136–38
Spectrogram, 120–22
Staff Dungeon, 99–102
Staff Wars, 97–99

Tonic Finder, 109–12

Rhythm Cat & Rhythm Cat 2, 71–73
Rhythm Maker, 36–38

Vocal Match, 80–82

Young Person's Guide to the Orchestra, 125–27

General Index

For the benefit of digital users, indexed terms that span two pages (e.g., 52–53) may, on occasion, appear on only one of those pages.

augmented reality, 152–56

classroom setups, 25–30
    1 device environments, 28–29
    1:1 device environments, 26–27
    1: multiple device environments, 27–28
    remote environments, 29–30
cognitive development, 4–5
Commercial-off-the-shelf (COTS) games, 21–23
Core Arts Standards, 13–15
    creating, 13
    connecting, 15
    performing, 14
    responding, 14
curriculum, 9–13
    SAMR Model, 9–11
    TPACK Model, 11–12
    Triple E Model, 12–13

edutainment games, 23–25
effective game design, 161–64

engagement and motivation, 6–7

lesson template description, 35–36

modding and coding, 148–51

online communities, 143–48

pedagogical approaches, 15–17
    Dalcroze Eurythmics, 17
    Kodály Method, 16–17
    Orff Schulwerk, 16
personal relevance, 5–6

scaffolding, 7–8
social-emotional learning, 8–9

troubleshooting, 30–33
    gaming controversies, 31–32
    teacher perspectives, 32–33
    technical issues, 31

virtual reality, 156–61

The manufacturer's authorised representative in the EU for product safety is Oxford
University Press España S.A. of El Parque Empresarial San Fernando de Henares,
Avenida de Castilla, 2 – 28830 Madrid (www.oup.es/en or product.safety@oup.com).
OUP España S.A. also acts as importer into Spain of products made by the manufacturer.

Printed in the USA/Agawam, MA
March 21, 2025

884675.014